RELIGIOUS DIVERSITY

'In this clear and accessible study of the major epistemic questions concerning religious diversity, Professor Basinger deals the final blow to the fashionable position that exclusivism is no longer intellectually credible.'
Marcel Sarot, University of Utrecht, The Netherlands

'Basinger's book provides a cutting-edge perspective on religious diversity. These arguments on issues ranging from the afterlife to philosophical pedagogy will provoke lively and illuminating debates.'
Kevin Meeker, University of South Alabama, USA

Religious diversity exists whenever seemingly sincere, knowledgeable individuals hold incompatible beliefs on the same religious issue. Diversity of this sort is pervasive, existing not only across basic theistic systems but also within these theistic systems themselves.

Religious Diversity explores the breadth and significance of such conflict. Examining the beliefs of various theistic systems, particularly within Christianity, Judaism, Hinduism and Buddhism, Basinger discusses seemingly incompatible claims about many religious issues, including the nature of God and the salvation of humankind. He considers particularly the work of Hick, Gellman, Plantinga, Schellenberg, Alston, Wainwright, and Quinn, applying their perspectives on 'exclusivism' and 'pluralism' as they become relevant to the issues in question.

Basinger's survey of the relevant literature, proposed solutions, and fresh insights offer an invaluable contribution not only for philosophers of religion and philosophical theologians but for anyone interested in the increasingly significant question of what a religious believer can or cannot justifiably say about their religious perspective.

ASHGATE PHILOSOPHY OF RELIGION SERIES

Series Editors

Paul Helm, Emeritus Professor of the History and Philosophy of
Religion, King's College London, UK
Jerome Gellman, Ben Gurion University of the Negev, Israel
Linda Zagzebski, University of Oklahoma, USA

Due to the work of Plantinga, Alston, Swinburne and others, the philosophy
of religion is now becoming recognized once again as a mainstream
philosophical discipline in which metaphysical, epistemological and moral
concepts and arguments are applied to issues of religious belief. The
Ashgate Philosophy of Religion Series fosters this resurgence of interest by
presenting a number of high profile titles spanning many critical debates,
and presenting new directions and new perspectives in contemporary
research and study. This new series presents books by leading international
scholars in the field, providing a platform for their own particular research
focus to be presented within a wider contextual framework. Offering
accessible, stimulating new contributions to each topic, this series will
prove of particular value and interest to academics, graduate, postgraduate
and upper-level undergraduate readers world-wide focusing on philosophy,
religious studies and theology, sociology or other related fields.

Religious Diversity

A philosophical assessment

DAVID BASINGER
Roberts Wesleyan College, New York, USA

Ashgate

Aldershot • Burlington USA • Singapore • Sydney

Published by
Ashgate Publishing Limited
Gower House
Croft Road
Aldershot
Hants GU11 3HR
England

Ashgate Publishing Company
131 Main Street
Burlington, VT 05401–5600 USA

Ashgate website: http://www.ashgate.com

British Library Cataloguing in Publication Data
Basinger, David
    Religious diversity: a philosophical assessment. –
    (Ashgate philosophy of religion series)
    1. Religions 2. Religion – Philosophy
    I. Title
    291

Library of Congress Cataloging-in-Publication Data
Basinger, David.
    Religious diversity: a philosophical assessment / David Basinger.
        p.cm. -- (Ashgate philosophy of religion series)
    Includes bibliographical references.
    ISBN 0-7546-1520-0 -- ISBN 0-7546-1521-9 (pbk.)
    1. Religious pluralism. 2. Religion -- Philosophy. 3. Knowledge, Theory of (Religion)
    I. Title. II. Series.

    BL85 .B365 2001
    291.1'72'01--dc21

2001022842

ISBN 0 7546 1520 0 (Cased)
ISBN 0 7546 1521 9 (Pbk)

This book is printed on acid free paper.
Typeset by Owain Hammonds, Bontgoch, Talybont, Ceredigion, Wales SY24 5DP.
Printed and bound in Great Britain by MPG Books Ltd, Bodmin, Cornwall.

Contents

Acknowledgements

Some of the material in this book first appeared (in more or less modified form) in previous publications of mine. Specifically, I have utilized material (with permission) from the following sources:

'Religious Diversity: Where Exclusivists Often Go Wrong', *International Journal for the Philosophy of Religion* 47 (2000): 43–55.

'The Challenge of Religious Diversity: A Middle Ground', *Sophia* 38/1 (March–April, 1999), pp. 41–53.

'Pluralism and Justified Religious Belief: A Response to Gellman', *Faith and Philosophy* 13 (1996), pp. 260–265.

'Divine Omniscience and the Soteriological Problem of Evil: Is the Type of Knowledge God Possesses Relevant?', *Religious Studies* 28 (1991), pp. 1–18.

'Plantinga, Pluralism and Justified Religious Belief', *Faith and Philosophy* 8 (January, 1991), pp. 67–80.

'Neutrality in the College Classroom: A Defense', *Faculty Dialogue* 12 (1989), pp. 79–92. Authored with Randall Basinger.

'Hick's Religious Pluralism and Reformed Epistemology', *Faith and Philosophy* 5 (1988), pp. 421–432.

Preface

As William James taught us, we are all forced to make significant decisions about the nature of reality. For instance, we talk and act as if we are more than simply material beings. But is this really so? We treat others as if they are morally responsible for their actions. However, are we really free in ways that allow for moral responsibility? And, if so, are there moral absolutes – moral principles that apply to all people at all times in all places?

This book is concerned with another of these basic metaphysical questions, namely whether there exists some form of supernatural reality – specifically some divine being or realm – with which we as humans are connected. My primary focus, however, is not ontological. That is, I do not consider the important question of whether there is, in fact, any divine reality. My focus is primarily epistemological: on what we can know or justifiably say about the nature of any such reality.

If all those who believed there to be some form of divine reality did, in fact, agree on the nature of this reality, then the main epistemic question would be quite straightforward: can we know or justifiably believe that such a reality actually exists? However, there is no such unanimity of thought on the nature of the divine. Rather, individuals of seemingly equal sincerity and knowledge conceive of the divine in a myriad of different, often incompatible ways. And the reality of such religious diversity generates another, even more fundamental epistemic question: if it is in fact the case that seemingly sincere, knowledgeable individuals differ on the nature of the divine, can the proponent of any specific perspective justifiably claim that she alone has the truth, or is at least closer to truth than all others?

In the pages that follow, I consider the current thinking of analytic philosophers of religion on this question, comparing and contrasting such thinking with my own. My objective, however, is not simply to contribute to the ongoing academic discussion. Since specific conceptualizations of the divine continue to influence significantly how individuals and groups (including nations) treat each other, it is also my hope that this book might in some way have a meaningful impact on how the actual proponents of specific religious perspectives respond to those with whom they disagree.

This book is the culmination of many years' work. And while many have made positive contributions to my thinking on these issues, I want specifically to acknowledge the influence of my brother, Randall, who from the time we were teens, building houses for our father, until now has been my primary sounding-board and critic. I also want to thank Linda Quinlan-Rus, a colleague whose editing expertise has been invaluable.

DB

vii

Chapter 1

Introduction

During my son's elementary school days, the halls were given the names of values students were to emulate. To get to my son's room, I started down Honesty Boulevard, took a left at Fairness Road and then finally turned onto Respect Lane. And although the parents in our school district continue to disagree on almost everything almost all of the time, I suspect that the school did not receive a single complaint about this clear attempt to promote a specific set of values in the school setting. The reason this is so, I assume, is that almost all of us, as parents, believe these values to be ones that children ought to learn and accept.

However, with respect to many, if not most issues – from those in sports to politics to religion – there usually do exist significant differences of opinion. Of course, as I will note in greater detail later, there are some contexts in which diversity of thought need cause us little epistemic concern. Sometimes a person – hopefully, for instance, a philosophy professor in a debate with undergraduate students in the classroom – clearly has access to more relevant information than do those with whom she disagrees. At other times – for instance, in the political arena – it may well be clear that those involved in a dispute know the truth but simply do not want to acknowledge it.

In many cases, though, epistemic conflicts persist among individuals who seem to be equally knowledgeable and sincere. Individuals who apparently have access to the same information and are equally interested in the truth affirm incompatible perspectives on, for instance, significant social issues such as capital punishment, physician-assisted suicide, and the status of same-sex relationships; on political issues such as the best form of government or the rights of children; and on economic issues such as the most productive type of economic system and the extent to which government should regulate private enterprise.

Such peer conflict, however, is nowhere more evident than in the area of religious thought. On almost every religious issue – from what God is like, to the extent to which God intervenes in earthly affairs, to how God would have us live, to what will happen when we die and how what we do now affects our eternal destiny – seemingly sincere, knowledgeable people differ significantly.

Religious epistemic peer conflict (hereafter in this chapter labelled religious diversity)[1] can fruitfully be explored in many ways – for instance, from psychological, anthropological or historical perspectives. I will, in this book, however, submit such diversity only to philosophical assessment. Specifically, I will attempt to identify the key issues that philosophers,

1

especially analytic philosophers of religion, are currently discussing, outline and critique the various perspectives on these issues, and offer a sustained argument for my own perspective.

The purpose of this chapter is to clarify the basic issues, outline the scope and method of my analysis, and share a brief summary of my conclusions.

Pervasiveness of Religious Diversity

I want first to emphasize the pervasiveness of religious diversity. It exists most notably at the level of basic theistic systems. For instance, while within Christianity, Judaism and Islam, it is believed that God is a personal deity, within Hinayana (Theravada) Buddhism God's existence is denied and within Hinduism the concept of a personal deity is, in an important sense, illusory. Within many forms of Christianity and Islam, the ultimate goal is subjective immortality in God's presence, while within Hinayana Buddhism the ultimate goal is the extinction of the self as a discrete, conscious entity.

However, significant, widespread diversity also exists *within* basic theistic systems. For example, within Christianity, believers differ significantly on the nature of God. Some see God as all-controlling, others as self-limiting and still others as incapable in principle of unilaterally controlling any aspect of reality. Some believe God to have infallible knowledge only of all that has occurred or is occurring, others claim God also has knowledge of all that will actually occur, while those who believe God possesses middle knowledge add that God knows all that would actually occur in any possible context.

Some believe the moral principles stipulated by God for correct human behaviour flow from God's nature and thus believe that these are also the principles that determine God's behaviour, while others believe that God plays by a different set of moral rules, that for God what is right is simply whatever God does. Some believe that only those who have consciously 'given their lives to Christ' will spend eternity in God's presence. Others believe that many who have never even heard the name of Jesus will enter God's presence, while others yet do not even believe subjective immortality (a conscious afterlife) to be a reality. Some believe, as do most in the Mennonite culture in which I was raised, that the Bible clearly teaches that the use of life-threatening force is always wrong, while others see clear biblical support for the use of force for self-defence and/or to preserve certain values.[2]

While no one will deny that the sorts of intra-system diversity I have just mentioned exist, it is quite popular in philosophical circles today to focus discussion primarily, if not solely, on diversity among basic theistic systems. However, I think this is a mistake. As I see it, the same basic questions that apply to inter-system diversity (for example, to differing perspectives on the most accurate basic theistic conception of God) apply just as clearly, and in exactly the same sense, to intra-system diversity (for example, to differing perspectives within Christianity over the extent of God's knowledge).

Moreover, as I will implicitly and explicitly argue throughout this book, the appropriate response to these questions – for example, the appropriate response to what we are obligated, or not obligated, to do when confronting diversity – is exactly the same for both types of diversity. And resolution, I will attempt to demonstrate, comes no easier with respect to intra-system diversity than it does at the inter-system level.

Furthermore, it is my belief that the practical import of intra-theistic diversity is just as significant as is that of inter-theistic diversity. For most Christians, for instance, the practical significance of retaining or modifying beliefs about God's power or knowledge is just as great as retaining or modifying the belief that Christianity is a better theistic explanatory hypothesis than is Islam.

Accordingly, I will in this book give equal emphasis to both types of diversity. I will at times center my discussion specifically on some aspect of inter-system diversity or intra-system diversity. However, in general, what I conclude about the nature of, and appropriate response to, religious diversity will apply to diversity of both types.

Scope of the Discussion

There has been a wide variety of responses to religious diversity – to the reality of conflicting religious truth claims. But there are two with which I will not concern myself. One obvious response to such diversity is to maintain that since there exists no divine reality – since the referent in such claims is non-existent – all such claims are false. However, while the actual existence of any form of divine reality remains a hotly contested issue within philosophical circles, this question is simply set aside in most current discussions of diversity, so I will do likewise.

Another possible response is what Joseph Runzo has labelled 'Religious Relativism'. This response is based on the assumption that 'truth itself is relative and plural'. Or to be more precise, it is based on the assumption that 'first-order truth-claims about reality – e.g., that a person or that a subatomic particle or that God exists – are relative to the world-view of a particular society'.[3] Applying this directly to the reality of conflicting religious truth claims, the religious relativist concludes that it is wrong to assume that at best one of a set of mutually incompatible religious claims about reality can be truth. What is accepted, rather, is the 'likelihood that more than one of the conflicting sets of *specific* truth-claims, which adherents of the differing world religions themselves regard as vital to their faith, is correct'.[4]

The debate between 'realist' and 'anti-realist' theories of truth is, of course, ongoing, and thus Religious Relativism is a perspective worthy of consideration. However, most current discussions of religious diversity presuppose a realist theory of truth. That is, it is normally presupposed, in

the words of William Alston, that 'religious beliefs are true or false
according to whether what is believed is the case, whether or not we have
any way of deciding this'.[5] Accordingly, given that the primary purpose of
this book is to assess the current thinking of analytic philosophers of
religion on questions of diversity, I will concern myself only with those
responses to diversity that assume there is a truth to the matter.

This leaves us with two basic responses to the reality of religious
diversity: religious exclusivism and religious pluralism. The most basic
distinction between these two perspectives is quite easy to state. The
exclusivist believes that one specific truth claim is correct, while the
pluralist believes that a number of literally incompatible truth claims
contain some truth. However, once we attempt to be more specific, we run
into significant ambiguity. Hence, it is important that I indicate as clearly as
possible the meanings of 'religious exclusivism' and 'religious pluralism'
with which I will be working.

Clarification of Key Terms

The phrase 'religious exclusivist' is sometimes used by philosophers such as
Peter van Inwagen as a label for anyone who claims that her perspective on a
religious issue is true (and, thus, that any incompatible perspective is false).[6]
In this sense, for example, anyone who claims that her perspective on the
question of who will spend eternity with God is true – whether that
perspective is that no one spends eternity with God, that the proponents of
only certain religions will spend eternity with God or that everyone will spend
eternity with God – is by virtue of this truth claim a religious exclusivist.
Looked at in this way, 'religious pluralism', however it is defined, is not a
competing position. Rather, an individual is either a religious exclusivist or
not. If a person believes that a given perspective on a religious issue is true,
then, regardless of the nature or content of that perspective, she is a religious
exclusivist; if a person doesn't hold such a belief, then she is not a religious
exclusivist with respect to the issue in question.

However, this is not normally the way in which 'religious exclusivism' is
defined in the literature. Usually, rather, the label 'religious exclusivist' is
reserved for someone who believes that one, and only one, of the many
incompatible basic theistic systems to which people have committed
themselves contains the truth. That is, this label is used to describe someone
who, in the words of Philip Quinn and Kevin Meeker, believes that 'one
religion is mostly right and all the other religions go seriously wrong',[7] or,
as restated by Runzo, believes that 'only one world religion is correct, and
all others are mistaken'.[8] Exclusivism, defined in this fashion, can be
contrasted meaningfully with 'religious pluralism', which, as Quinn and
Meeker rightly note, is most often the label given the view that 'all the
major religious traditions – the so-called world religions – are in contact
with the same ultimate religious reality' and thus offer different, but equally
efficacious access, to the divine.[9]

In short, given this definition of exclusivism, it is not simply the affirmation of a religious truth claim that makes one a religious exclusivist. It is, rather, the nature of this truth claim. If the claim is that one, and only one, basic theistic perspective offers an accurate description of reality, then the person making such a claim is a religious exclusivist. If the claim is that many basic theistic perspectives offer equal access to the truth, then the person is a religious pluralist.

There are, it should be noted, variations of both religious exclusivism and pluralism (defined in this manner). For instance, Keith Ward distinguishes between hard pluralism – the view that many of the main religious traditions do not actually contain mutually exclusive beliefs and thus can be considered in their present state to be equally valid paths to the divine – and soft pluralism – the view that although many of the main religions do actually contain mutually exclusive religious beliefs, the divine can manifest itself in many religious traditions and humans can respond appropriately to the divine in all such traditions.[10]

There is also a well-known distinction between hard exclusivism and inclusivism (soft exclusivism). The hard exclusivist claims the divine can be accessed through one, and only one, religious perspective; the inclusivist maintains that while *full* access to the divine is possible through one, and only one, religious perspective, partial or selective access is possible through other perspectives. So, for instance, while the Christian hard exclusivist will claim that only 'true Christians' can actually experience God now, the Christian inclusivist will claim that although only true Christians can experience God to the greatest extent possible, proponents of other religions can actually experience God to varying degrees. And while the Christian hard exclusivist claims that only those who have 'accepted Christ' (and possibly 'children') can spend eternity with God, the Christian inclusivist claims that although those who have accepted Christ will spend eternity with God, it may well be that some who have not accepted Christ will also spend eternity with God as the result of meeting other sufficient conditions a just God has stipulated for them.[11]

I will, when assessing the views of others, work with whatever definitions they utilize. However, the definitions for 'exclusivism' and 'pluralism' I prefer, and thus will utilize whenever possible, differ in a meaningful sense from those offered by most. If forced to choose between the more general epistemic interpretation of religious exclusivism sometimes offered by those such as van Inwagen and the narrower, more standard interpretation of religious exclusivism offered by those such as Quinn and Meeker, I prefer the latter. But both, it seems to me, are deficient in one respect. In both cases it is assumed that religious diversity exists only in relation to different basic theistic systems. Quinn and Meeker, for instance, actually use as their working definition of religious diversity 'the undisputed fact that different religions espouse doctrines that are at least apparently in conflict and offer alternative paths of salvation and liberation'.[12] There is in neither case recognition of the type of intra-system diversity that I have argued is so pervasive and important.

Furthermore, I am uncomfortable with the 'all-or-nothing' approach implicit in the standard distinction between exclusivism and pluralism, even when their variants are acknowledged. The implicit assumption is that one is *either* some form of exclusivist *or* some form of pluralist. However, this seems to me to be a false dilemma. For instance, I sometimes have students who are hard exclusivists with respect to the question of who can spend eternity with God, but are pluralists with respect to the question of who can experience God's presence now. So the terms in question, I believe, need to be applied on a case-by-case basis.[13]

However, while I find it easy to criticize the definitions offered by others, I also find it difficult to formulate alternatives that capture the exact distinctions I believe important. It does seem to me, though, that the following will serve as adequate working definitions for what I see as the three most important concepts with which we will be concerned: religious exclusivism, religious non-exclusivism and religious pluralism. For the purpose of our discussion, someone is a religious exclusivist with respect to a given issue when she believes the doctrinal perspective of only one basic theistic system (for instance, only one of the major world religions) or only one of the doctrinal variants within a basic theistic system (for instance, only Christianity) to be the truth or at least closer to the truth than any other doctrinal perspective on this issue.[14] Someone is a religious non-exclusivist with respect to a given issue when she denies that the doctrinal perspective of any basic theistic system or variant thereof is superior to all other doctrinal perspectives on this issue. And someone is a religious pluralist with respect to a given issue when she claims not only (as a non-exclusivist) that no specific doctrinal perspective is superior but also makes the positive claim that the doctrinal perspectives of more than one basic theistic system or variant thereof are equally close to the truth.

For instance, with respect to the question of what conditions must be met before one can spend eternity in God's presence, someone who claimed that only by meeting certain Christian or certain Muslim criteria can one enter God's presence would be an exclusivist on this issue. Someone who, though religious, denied that we as humans are in a position to identify the relevant criteria would be a religious non-exclusivist. And someone who claimed that the criteria of many different religious traditions are sufficient would be a religious pluralist with respect to the question at hand.[15]

Summary of Remaining Chapters

There are, of course, many specific topics on which our philosophical discussion of religious diversity could focus. We could, for instance, consider the manner in which the reality of religious diversity influenced the philosophical thought of key philosophers, such as Descartes, Kant and Hume. Or we could consider the manner in which religious believers actually do respond to the diversity they encounter. However, current philosophical discussions focus almost exclusively on epistemic issues. Specifically, as I see it, most current discussions focus on two basic questions:

(1) Can the religious exclusivist simply ignore religious diversity with epistemic impunity, or does the reality of such diversity place the exclusivist under certain epistemic obligations?
(2) Assuming an epistemic response to diversity is required or desired, is it justifiable for an exclusivist to continue to maintain, in the face of such diversity, that her specific perspective is superior?

Accordingly, what follows in subsequent chapters will focus on issues of this type.[16]

In Chapter 2, I consider whether the recognition of diversity requires anything of a religious believer. Specifically, I consider the basic epistemic question of whether the reality of diversity places the religious exclusivist under any type of epistemic obligation, and, if so, whether she is required in response only to defend her current perspective or also to attempt to resolve the conflict(s) at hand. After explaining why I believe that acknowledged diversity does indeed place the exclusivist under an obligation to attempt to resolve the dispute in question, I argue that even those who want to deny that the exclusivist is under such an obligation should at least admit that there exist good reasons for the exclusivist to engage in the type of belief assessment that will allow her to be assured that her perspective really is worthy of continued affirmation.

In Chapter 3, I discuss the epistemic status of the religious exclusivist who agrees that acknowledged diversity requires (or at least strongly invites) belief assessment, but also believes (along with most philosophers of religion) that such assessment will not result in an objective adjudication of the competing claims. Specifically, I consider whether the exclusivist, under these conditions, can continue justifiably to affirm her exclusivist perspective. After considering the perspectives of William Alston and his critics, I concur with Alston's basic contention that although only one of a set of incompatible exclusivistic perspectives on a given religious issue can in fact be correct, proponents of each perspective can, in principle, justifiably continue to maintain that they alone have the truth.

Chapter 4 moves from the question of whether the religious exclusivist is justified in retaining her exclusivistic perspective in the face of diversity to the question of whether it is plausible or reasonable for her to do so. Specifically, this chapter is an assessment of the influential work of John Hick, who argues that the consideration of certain factors – for example, the fact that most people affirm the religious perspective of the culture in which they were raised or the fact that most of the world's great religions have equal transformational efficacy – makes the contention that many competing religious perspectives on a given issue are equally close to the truth (a pluralistic response) much more plausible than the contention that one perspective is superior (an exclusivistic response).

In response, I grant that the factors Hick cites do pose a *prima facie* challenge to exclusivistic belief and thus give the exclusivist good reason to engage in belief assessment in the face of diversity. However, while such assessment may well result in pared-down exclusivistic theologies or a conversion to pluralism, Hick has not, I contend, made pluralism the inevitable, or even the more plausible, choice.

In Chapter 5, I turn to the consideration of a specific religious issue that continues to be the focus of much debate in philosophical circles: the traditional exclusivistic Christian claim that while 'true Christians' will spend eternity in a state of conscious bliss with God (heaven), many, if not most non-Christians (except possibly for children) will spend eternity in a conscious state of damnation (hell). Specifically, I outline and assess various attempts by traditional exclusivists to clarify and/or defend the claim in question, with special emphasis on William Craig's contention that granting God middle knowledge – granting God the ability to know what will in fact happen in every conceivable context – allows the exclusivist to claim both that many will spend eternity apart from God and yet that God is just and fair. I conclude that while there exist good reasons for a salvific exclusivist to reassess her contention that those who don't affirm her specific religious perspective will spend eternity apart from God, this is a claim that such an exclusivist can, in the last analysis, justifiably affirm.

Chapter 6 considers the relationship between exclusivism and apologetics. Most philosophers agree that exclusivists not only can, but should, engage in negative apologetics – that is, attempt to defend their right to remain exclusivists. However, most exclusivists, like their pluralistic counterparts, also try to convince others that they are right. That is, they, like most pluralists, engage in what has come to be called positive apologetics. And the question of whether exclusivists can, and if so should, engage in this form of apologetical activity remains a debatable issue. After rejecting the arguments of those who claim that exclusivists cannot justifiably engage in such activity, I argue that whether or not a given exclusivist is obligated to try to convert others to her perspective depends on if such proselytization is a requirement within the basic theistic system to which she is committed.

Finally, in Chapter 7, I explore the relationship between religious diversity and teaching. Specifically, I argue that the reality of epistemic diversity – the fact that sincere, equally knowledgeable individuals differ on almost every issue that philosophers discuss – is one of the primary reasons why the philosopher *qua* teacher ought to keep her personal opinion out of the classroom.

Practical Significance of Current Diversity

Before turning to our first topic, one final comment is in order. As already noted, philosophical interest in religious diversity is not new. The reality of such diversity was in part responsible for important work by such figures as Descartes, Hume and Kant. Moreover, such diversity clearly remains of theoretical interest to philosophers today, primarily I think because of the current emphasis on justified or warranted belief initiated by prominent philosophers of religion such as Alvin Plantinga and William Alston.[17]

However, the increasing practical significance of religious diversity cannot, I believe, be overemphasized. The technological advances of the past century continue to give us ever-increasing, immediate, first-hand access to other cultural perspectives, including a wide range of diverse religious perspectives. And given such exposure, it is becoming increasingly difficult for any religious believer to avoid the question of whether she should continue to consider her basic theistic system superior to all others. Furthermore, there are important debates over core beliefs – for instance, over God's nature – within many, if not most, basic theistic systems. Consequently, the issues discussed in this book are not simply of academic interest. Such issues – especially those related to epistemic obligation – are of practical significance for the thought and behaviour of actual believers.[18]

Notes

1. I personally believe 'religious epistemic peer conflict' to be a more adequate descriptor than 'religious diversity' for the type of epistemic tension with which this book is concerned. However, since the majority of philosophers currently prefer 'religious diversity', I, too, will use this descriptor except in those contexts where I believe 'religious epistemic peer conflict' to be clearly preferable.
2. While this is not a book about Judeo-Christian diversity alone, the majority of examples will center around such diversity for two reasons: this is the religious perspective with which I am most familiar, and it is the religious perspective most often considered by analytic philosophers in this context. The general principles being discussed, though, will normally apply to other basic religious perspectives as well.
3. Joseph Runzo, 'God, Commitment, and Other Faiths: Pluralism vs. Relativism', *Faith and Philosophy* 5 (October 1988), p. 351.
4. Runzo, p. 357.
5. William Alston, 'Religious Diversity and Perceptual Knowledge of God', *Faith and Philosophy* 5 (October 1988), p. 434.
6. Peter van Inwagen, 'A Reply to Professor Hick', *Faith and Philosophy* 14 (July 1997), p. 300. Alvin Plantinga sometimes offers an analogous argument: that alleged nonexclusivists also make exclusivistic claims. See, for example, Plantinga, 'Pluralism: A Defense of Exclusivism', in *The Philosophical Challenge of Religious Diversity*, eds Kevin Meeker and Philip L. Quinn (New York: Oxford University Press, 2000), pp. 177–79.
7. Meeker and Quinn, p. 3.
8. Runzo, p. 346.
9. Meeker and Quinn, p. 3. Runzo offers us an even more precise definition of this sort: a religious pluralist is someone who maintains that 'ultimately all world religions are correct, each offering a different salvific path and partial perspective *vis-à-vis* the one Ultimate Reality' (p. 347).
10. Keith Ward, 'Truth and the Diversity of Religions', in *The Philosophical Challenge of Religious Diversity*, pp. 123–4.
11. For helpful discussions of the distinction between hard exclusivism and inclusivism, see Michael Peterson, William Hasker, Bruce Reichenbach and David Basinger, *Reason and Religious Belief: An Introduction to the Philosophy of Religion*, 2nd edn. (New York: Oxford Press, 1998), pp. 259–278, and Peterson et al., *Philosophy of Religion: Selected Readings* (New York: Oxford Press, 1996), pp. 493–526.

12. Meeker and Quinn, p. 3.
13. Andrew Koehl is another philosopher who recognizes this distinction. See his 'Reformed Epistemology and Diversity', forthcoming in *Faith and Philosophy*.
14. I do not want to give the impression that I am the only philosopher defining religious exclusivism in terms of specific beliefs. Andrew Koehl does so also: 'One who holds an [exclusivistic belief] is what we might call a doctrinal exclusivist with respect to that belief. She maintains that her belief is true and that others incompatible with it are false' ('Reformed Epistemology and Diversity').
15. These definitions are still more ambiguous than I would like. For example, if we consider religious pluralism to be a basic theistic system, then religious pluralists again become religious exclusivists, given my definition of exclusivism. But I hope that these definitions are clear enough to point to the basic distinctions I have in mind.
16. I am not limiting the scope of my discussion in this fashion because I think that philosophers, especially analytic philosophers, necessarily offer the best approach to the question of religious diversity. But analytic philosophers are, I believe, asking questions of theoretical and practical significance worthy of focused consideration.
17. Alston's most significant work in this regard is *Perceiving God: The Epistemology of Religious Experience* (Ithaca: Cornell University Press, 1991); Plantinga's most significant work is *Warranted Christian Belief* (New York: Oxford Press, 2000).
18. It is important to note that my discussion will center on the justification of religious belief and not on the authenticity of religious experience. Whether there is a spiritual reality and whether any given individual is in fact in some sort of relationship with such a reality are important questions with which I will not be concerned in this book. I will restrict myself to the consideration of what a religious believer can or cannot justifiably say about God or her religious perspective, especially given the reality of religious diversity.

Chapter 2

Diversity and Epistemic Obligation

In Chapter 1, I argued that pervasive, significant diversity (epistemic peer conflict) exists both among basic theistic systems and within such systems. How, though, ought the proponent of a specific religious perspective – the religious exclusivist – respond to such diversity? How ought the proponent of Judaism, for example, respond to the fact that seemingly sincere, knowledgeable individuals maintain that Christianity or Islam is the correct perspective? Or how ought the Christian, who believes the Bible to teach that God ultimately controls all, including free choice, respond to the fact that many seemingly sincere, knowledgeable fellow Christians believe the Bible to teach that God has voluntarily given up control in those cases where freedom has been granted, or believe that God cannot unilaterally control any state of affairs since all entities always possess some degree of self-determination *vis-à-vis* God?[1]

My Position

My basic response to this question, which has previously been labeled 'Basinger's Rule', is the following: 'If a religious exclusivist wants to maximize truth and avoid error, she is under a *prima facie* obligation to attempt to resolve significant epistemic peer conflict'.[2] To avoid unnecessary confusion, let me be more specific about what I am and am not intending here. First, Basinger's Rule is a conditional claim. I am claiming that *if* an exclusivist desires to maximize truth and avoid error, she is under the obligation in question. This qualification is important because sometimes a person has no desire to maximize truth in the face of epistemic conflict.[3] For instance, I suspect that the main reason I do not videotape myself in the classroom is because I really do not want to know how I perform. I am happier with the image of myself as a good teacher that I have created. Sometimes, however, the truth does matter to us – for example, when we are attempting to identify the cause of health problems – and when this is the case for a religious exclusivist (which I hope is often), then I continue to believe she is under the obligation in question.

Second, let me explain what I mean by 'epistemic peer conflict'. As I am using this phrase, we face epistemic peer conflict only in those contexts in which we have no objective reason to doubt that those with whom we disagree are (1) equally knowledgeable, that is, have access to as much relevant information as we do, and (2) equally sincere, that is, desire as much as we do to affirm what is true.[4] I have no obligation to attempt to resolve a conflict over the merits of given cars with a showroom salesperson because I have good reason to believe that he is much less interested in which car actually is best than in selling me the car that will make him the most profit. And I feel little obligation to attempt to resolve an interpretational conflict between the author of a well-respected text on Plato's work and the first-year student who has never even read the relevant primary texts since I do not consider the student to be equally knowledgeable. In short, the mere fact that others disagree with a religious exclusivist does not place her under the obligation that I have in mind. Basinger's Rule holds *only* in those contexts in which the exclusivist has no reason to doubt that those with whom she disagrees really are on equal epistemic footing.

Third, let me clarify what I mean when I claim that the religious exclusivist who faces epistemic peer conflict is obligated to 'attempt to resolve' it. When I initially proposed Basinger's Rule, I emphasized that exclusivists (of any sort) facing such conflict should, as a general rule, first attempt to resolve the tension on evidential grounds.[5] I still believe that in many contexts this is the most fruitful way to proceed. If two students who want to do well on a major exam have differing recollections of when the exam is to be given, then I believe they are obligated to consider what relevant evidence there is – the syllabus, the recollections of others in the class, what the professor says if contacted – in an attempt to resolve this conflict. Moreover, I believe that, in cases such as this, resolution can normally be achieved.

However, I have always maintained, and continue to hold, that there seldom exists an objective evidential basis for resolving epistemic conflicts in the religious realm.[6] Thus, while I still believe that the consideration of relevant evidence can help clarify, and possibly in some cases even minimize, religious epistemic peer conflict, my emphasis when applying Basinger's Rule to conflicts of this type is not on evidential resolution. What I want to maintain, rather, is that even when there is good reason to believe that no objective resolution to epistemic peer conflict will be forthcoming, a religious exclusivist is still obligated to 'attempt to resolve' the tension in question in the sense that she has an obligation to identify and assess the reasons why she and her epistemic competitors hold the beliefs they do.[7]

For example, consider the debate surrounding the extent of God's knowledge, which I see as a dispute among equally knowledgeable, sincere theists. I seriously doubt that there exists any objective basis – either philosophical or theological – for the resolution of this epistemic conflict. Yet I want to claim that if those exclusivists involved in this dispute really desire the truth, they still have an obligation to identify and assess the reasons why they, and those with whom they disagree, hold their respective positions.

Fourth, let me say a little about the relationship between Basinger's Rule and justified belief. There is a sense in which I believe that the religious exclusivist who, in the face of epistemic peer conflict, fails to meet this obligation – fails to submit the belief(s) in question to belief assessment – is no longer justified in claiming that her perspective is superior. However, it is important that I specify in exactly what sense I believe this is true. I am not arguing that a religious exclusivist, even one who acknowledges epistemic peer conflict, must actually have met the obligation in question before she can justifiably continue to maintain her perspective is superior. There may be many legitimate reasons why a religious exclusivist cannot immediately or ever discharge this duty. She may, for instance, not have the time or psychological resources to do so. This is why I say Basinger's Rule is a *prima facie* obligation.

However, almost everyone agrees that a person who consciously violates an epistemic duty forfeits justified belief. Moreover, it seems to me that choosing not to assess a belief that is the subject of epistemic peer conflict is choosing not to maximize truth and maximizing truth is a basic epistemic duty. So I do believe that once a religious exclusivist acknowledges epistemic peer conflict, for her to choose then to retain a purely defensive posture – for her to then claim she is under no obligation to consider the matter further – is for her to forfeit her right to claim justifiably that her perspective is superior.[8]

Finally, on a related note, let me clarify what I think such assessment must produce for the religious exclusivist to retain justified belief. On the basis of what has already been said, it should be obvious that I do not mean to imply by Basinger's Rule that an exclusivist must demonstrate superiority in relation to some set of objective criteria – criteria accepted by all parties in the dispute – before she can justifiably retain her perspective. Rather, I believe, in general, that a religious exclusivist can justifiably retain her exclusivistic perspective unless belief assessment gives her reason to (or simply brings it about that she does in fact) modify or abandon her current perspective. Specifically, I continue to believe that the truth-seeking exclusivist who has submitted her relevant beliefs to serious assessment is justified in continuing to maintain that her perspective is superior if, after such assessment, she still finds herself believing the evidence for her perspective to be most compelling, or finds her subjective experience confirming her beliefs, or simply finds that her perspective best organizes and explains the relevant components of reality.[9]

Ought Basinger's Rule be accepted? Is it really true, as I claim, that if a religious exclusivist desires to maximize truth and avoid error, she is obligated to identify and assess the relevant beliefs in the face of epistemic peer conflict? While my position is open to debate at many points, I will focus my attention in this chapter on what I see as the two most significant challenges offered to date: those set forth by Alvin Plantinga and Jerome Gellman.[10]

Plantinga's Challenge

Plantinga does not take the potential impact of religious epistemic peer conflict lightly. In his most recent work, he acknowledges that 'for many or most exclusivists, I think, the enormous variety of human religious response' can directly reduce 'level of confidence or degree of belief ... and it may even deprive us of some of the comfort and peace the Lord has promised his followers'.[11] Yet although 'things *could* go this way', he tells us, 'they *needn't* go this way'. 'A fresh or heightened awareness of the facts of religious pluralism could bring about a reappraisal of one's religious life, a reawakening, a new or renewed and deepened grasp and apprehension' of one's exclusivistic beliefs. And this may well cause one to come to believe even more firmly in these beliefs.[12]

It seems clear to me, therefore, that Plantinga does not hold the concept of belief assessment central to 'Basinger's Rule' to be inherently flawed. When the acknowledgement of epistemic peer conflict brings a proponent of a specific religious perspective into a certain psychological state – one of doubt or uncertainty – then, as I am reading Plantinga, such a person may well need, or even be unable not, to engage in serious belief assessment designed to resolve the conflict in question.

Plantinga also seems to agree with my claim that *if* a proponent of a specific religious perspective has no reason to doubt that those with whom she disagrees really are on equal epistemic footing, then she is under a *prima facie* obligation to attempt to resolve the conflict, regardless of how 'psychologically troubling' this conflict is for her personally. At least that is what I take him to mean when he acknowledges, in another context, that *if* an exclusivist did agree that the beliefs of others were 'as epistemically well-based as his own, then perhaps he would indeed be arbitrary' in holding them without further consideration.[13]

However, Plantinga has claimed, and apparently still believes, that the exclusivist need never acknowledge that she is facing true epistemic parity – need never admit that she actually is differing with true epistemic peers. An exclusivist, he begins, can clearly acknowledge that 'the views of others seem just as true to them as hers do to her; they have all the same internal markers as her own. She may agree further that these others are *justified*, flouting no epistemic duty, in believing as they do. She may agree still further that she doesn't know of any arguments that would convince them that they are wrong and she is right'.[14]

However, our exclusivist, Plantinga continues, is still likely to believe that 'he has been epistemically favored in some way'. For instance, if he is a Christian exclusivist, he might believe that he has been graced by 'the Internal Witness of the Holy Spirit; or perhaps he thinks the Holy Spirit preserves the Christian church from serious error, at least with respect to the fundamentals of Christian belief; or perhaps he thinks that he has been converted by divine grace, so that he now sees what before was obscure to him – a blessing not so far bestowed upon the dissenters'.[15]

Moreover, if any of these beliefs are true, Plantinga contends, then the Christian is quite probably 'in a better position, epistemically speaking, than those who reject Christian belief'. Thus, since it cannot be demonstrated that Christian belief is very likely false, the Christian remains justified, he concludes, in maintaining that the proponents of other religious perspectives are not actually on equal epistemic footing.[16]

In response, I grant that the epistemic obligation in Basinger's Rule – the obligation to engage in belief assessment – arises only when such conflict is between or among epistemic peers. Thus, if, as Plantinga argues, the religious exclusivist can maintain justifiably that those with whom she disagrees are not her peers, then the exclusivist can justifiably deny that such assessment is a necessary condition for continuing to hold her exclusivistic perspective to be superior.

However, I deny that the exclusivist can justifiably claim her epistemic competitors are not her epistemic peers in the sense of epistemic parity intended in Basinger's Rule. I do not deny that most exclusivists do in fact believe themselves to be in an epistemically superior position, nor do I even deny that they are justified in doing so. However, Basinger's Rule should not be read as requiring that an exclusivist engage in belief assessment only when it can be demonstrated that those who affirm beliefs incompatible with hers *actually are* on equal epistemic footing. Basinger's Rule is meant to shift the burden of proof to the exclusivist. What is required of an exclusivist, as I intend it, is that she engage in belief assessment unless she can demonstrate on epistemic grounds that are (or should be) accepted by all rational people that proponents of the other perspectives *are not actually* on equal epistemic footing. And Plantinga himself clearly believes that religious exclusivists often find themselves in this epistemic situation.[17]

Why, though, should any of this be of concern to Plantinga? He might well acknowledge that my understanding of epistemic parity does shift the burden of proof but argue that I have offered no basis, other than personal preference, for why he ought to agree – for why he does not remain justified in retaining the concept of epistemic parity with which he is working. That is, Plantinga might grant that I am personally justified in maintaining that an exclusivist must engage in the type of belief assessment outlined in Basinger's Rule unless she can demonstrate on objective epistemic grounds that proponents of the other perspectives *are not actually* on equal epistemic footing, but argue that unless I can offer some reason why he cannot justifiably disagree, we have here simply a difference of opinion.

I grant that if what we have here is simply a difference of opinion, then Basinger's Rule can justifiably be rejected. However, I believe there to be a good reason to favour my understanding of epistemic parity – my reading of who shoulders the burden of proof in this context. The essence of Plantinga's position, I think, can be fairly summarized in the following epistemic parity principle (EPP):

> Even if I grant that those with whom I disagree on a given issue are justified in believing as they do, if it cannot be demonstrated that either my perspective or my explanation for why others disagree is very likely false, I remain justified in maintaining that those with whom I disagree are not actually on equal epistemic footing and, thus, in denying that belief assessment is a necessary condition for justifiably retaining my exclusivistic perspective.

Plantinga applies EPP solely to disputes between or among basic theistic systems – specifically, to the tension between Christian and non-Christian perspectives. However, as I have already argued, I see no justifiable reason why the question of how an exclusivist ought to respond to epistemic peer conflict should be restricted to inter-system debates. We must also consider how the proponent of a basic theistic system ought to respond when facing incompatible beliefs within this system. And, when we do, I think Plantinga's contention that the exclusivist can, based on EPP, justifiably deny that her competitors are on equal epistemic footing becomes dubious.

Consider, for instance, the differing perspectives on God's power held by those Christian theological determinists who believe that God retains total control over all states of affairs, including the free choices of humans, and those Christian freewill theists who believe that to the extent that God grants humans freedom, God gives up control over the choices made.[18]

Using Plantinga's line of reasoning – applying EPP – it seems to me a theological determinist could argue as follows: I acknowledge that the perspective on God's power held by freewill theists seems just as true to them as mine does to me; their beliefs have all the same internal markers as my own. I agree further that freewill theists are justified, flouting no epistemic duty, in believing as they do. I agree still further that I don't know of any arguments that would convince them that they are wrong and I am right.

However, I still believe that I am in an epistemically favoured position. The Internal Witness of the Holy Spirit convinces me that my perspective is the correct Christian perspective on this issue. I am not in a position to see why freewill theists believe otherwise. Perhaps they are not yet open to the truth, or perhaps the Spirit has for some reason not yet helped them to see the truth clearly. Still, I do firmly believe that the truth on this issue is not clearly evident to them.

Thus, since it cannot be demonstrated that either my perspective, or my explanation for why freewill theists disagree, is very likely false, I remain justified in maintaining that freewill theists are not actually on equal epistemic footing and, accordingly, remain justified in denying that belief assessment is a necessary condition for continuing to maintain that my perspective is superior to that of freewill theists.[19]

Does, however, the exclusivist really want EPP applied to intra-system disputes such as this? Does she really want to say that all that is required of disputants in an intra-system debate is that they play defence – that they defend what they already believe from potential defeaters? Does she really want to say that our disputants need not attempt to understand why they or their competitors hold the beliefs they do, that they need not seriously consider the possibility that their competitors may be correct, or that some compromise may be possible given further discussion? I don't think so.

First of all, many exclusivists are intra-system, as well as inter-system, proselytizers. That is, many times an exclusivist doesn't want only to convince proponents of other basic theistic systems to see things her way. She also often wants to convince those within her own basic system who disagree with her on doctrinal issues to accept her perspective. Moreover, in this intra-system effort, she almost always urges those with whom she is in dialogue to consider comparatively the differing perspectives in question.

That is, she clearly encourages those with whom she disagrees *not* to refrain from assessing their beliefs – not to believe that all that they need to do is play defence. And I don't see how an exclusivist can with integrity do so if EPP is accepted as a general epistemic response to peer conflict.

Second, within most religious settings, serious discussion of disputed doctrinal issues is encouraged. Many Christians, for instance, believe the Bible to recommend, if not command, thoughtful discussion of any intra-system conflict. And the implicit assumption on which this sort of discussion is almost always based is not only that participants be open to alternative points of view but that they also be willing to modify their own – that they be willing to do what EEP claims they need not.

Moreover, as will be discussed in greater detail later in this chapter, almost all exclusivists have, as a matter of fact, modified doctrinal beliefs as the result of belief assessment triggered by the assumption that those with whom they disagreed on a given intra-system issue were equally knowledgeable and sincere, that they were on equal epistemic footing. And, since most of these exclusivists remain convinced that such belief modification was not only appropriate but beneficial, it is difficult to see why they would want to accept EEP as a general epistemic principle – would want to accept a principle that claims that they need not have engaged in the type of belief assessment that produced the modification in question.

None of this, I grant, is a conclusive argument against the affirmation of EPP – against the claim that since those with whom we disagree cannot demonstrate that our explanation for why they differ with us is false, we can justifiably deny they are our epistemic peers and thus justifiably refrain from engaging in belief assessment. An exclusivist could, as far as I can tell, justifiably affirm this principle, and on that basis, reject the obligation for belief assessment under which I claim Basinger's Rule places the proponent of a specific religious perspective who becomes aware of peer conflict over significant issues.

However, once we recognize that EPP applies to intra-system peer conflict as well as to inter-system peer conflict – to seeming conflict between or among the beliefs of proponents of a basic theistic system as well as to seeming conflict between or among the beliefs of proponents of differing basic theistic systems – I believe we can see that EPP is a principle that most exclusivists either reject or fail to apply consistently. Accordingly, I deny that Plantinga and I have simply a difference of opinion over Basinger's Rule. The exclusivist, I think I have shown, has good reason to side with me.[20]

Gellman's Initial Challenge

But even if I am correct, Basinger's Rule – my contention that exclusivists ought to engage in belief assessment in the face of peer conflict (diversity) – faces a set of formidable challenges from Jerome Gellman. One challenge centers on what Gellman identifies as *rock bottom religious beliefs*. Rock bottom beliefs, as he defines them, are the governors or guardians of epistemic systems. They are the epistemic givens – the assumed, foundational truths – upon which all else is built. As such, they are beliefs that 'determine the acceptability of belief candidates, while [not themselves being] subject to deeper epistemic justification'.[21] Or, stated differently yet, once beliefs become rock bottom (regardless of how they were initially formed) they no longer function as grounded beliefs, but as grounding beliefs. They are no longer vulnerable to assessment, but instead are the starting points of assessment.

Not surprisingly, therefore, Gellman concludes that Basinger's Rule is too strong. He seems to grant that if a religious belief affirmed by an exclusivist is *not* rock bottom (or not a logical consequent of a belief that is rock bottom), then it may well be subject to this epistemic principle. However, if a religious belief that is the subject of peer conflict *is* rock bottom for an exclusivist, Gellman argues, to attempt to resolve the conflict is superfluous. Since belief assessment only makes sense when one isn't certain that the belief in question is true, and since rock bottom religious beliefs are among the foundational truths – the basic, assumed truths – in an exclusivist's epistemic system, no assessment is necessary. Rather, given the epistemic status of rock bottom beliefs, when an exclusivist encounters a challenge to such a belief – for example, a challenge to her rock bottom belief in God's ultimate control over all earthly affairs – she can justifiably utilize the G.E. Moore switch. That is, she can justifiably maintain that because her rock bottom belief is true, the competing belief can be rejected.

Or, to state Gellman's point in terms more directly related to my explication of Basinger's Rule, it is my contention that if an exclusivist is committed to truth, epistemic peer conflict mandates belief assessment. Gellman's response is that if a belief facing peer challenge is in an exclusivist's set of rock bottom beliefs, then she can justifiably consider this belief true and thus immune from any need for assessment, even if she cannot demonstrate that her epistemic opponent is not on equal epistemic footing.

In response to Gellman's challenge, let me first identify our points of agreement. I agree that exclusivists do actually possess and utilize what Gellman calls rock bottom beliefs. That is, I agree that at any given time, exclusivists do possess certain foundational beliefs that stand as guardians of their belief systems, beliefs that at that point determine what else can be considered true, what else can be allowed. Many of my students, for instance, simply believe that God exists or God is good or God is all-controlling and interpret everything else in light of such beliefs.

However, it is one thing to acknowledge that someone holds (indeed must hold) rock bottom beliefs, and something quite different to say that such beliefs are justifiably immune from assessment, especially in the face of epistemic peer conflict. Accordingly, the key question, as I see it, is not whether religious exclusivists do possess rock bottom beliefs or even whether they can justifiably do so. The key question is whether rock bottom beliefs can justifiably be considered immune from Basinger's Rule – can justifiably be considered immune from belief assessment. Gellman believes the answer to be yes; I disagree.

However, I am going to refrain at present from arguing that religious exclusivists are *obligated* to assess even rock bottom beliefs when faced with peer conflict and defend instead a somewhat weaker claim: that in the face of epistemic peer conflict religious exclusivists should at least recognize the considerable epistemic value in assessing their beliefs, especially those that are rock bottom.

Let me explain why I am adopting this strategy. I often impress on my students the fact that when someone attempts to defend a very strong, controversial claim, this person runs the risk of allowing her opponents to avoid the consideration of less controversial variants. For example, if someone attempts to argue that we are all obligated to give blood or donate organs, she allows others to challenge this claim and therefore avoid consideration of the less controversial claim that giving blood and donating organs are very valuable, praiseworthy activities that we all ought to consider seriously.

The same point, I believe, is relevant in our discussion. I continue to believe that Basinger's Rule describes a basic epistemic obligation, even with respect to rock bottom beliefs. However, if I argue only this point, then I allow those who believe we are under no such obligation to avoid what I see as an important related question: even if an exclusivist is not obligated to assess her rock bottom religious beliefs in the face of epistemic peer conflict, are there good reasons why she should 'voluntarily' do so?

The answer to this question, I believe, is clearly yes. As I have repeatedly stated, I do not deny that religious exclusivists hold rock bottom religious beliefs. But there is, in fact, something quite odd or surprising about such beliefs. Since rock bottom beliefs are, by definition, not subject to question, we might expect that once beliefs have acquired this epistemic designation, they would retain it indefinitely. As a matter of fact, though, this is not the case. In actual practice, not all beliefs that are rock bottom at a given point in time actually do remain so.

I base this claim primarily on my own experience. In my 27 years of teaching, I have had about 8,000 students of all ages, types, and religious perspectives. And I have had almost all of them engage in the following thought experiment. Think, I ask them, of beliefs you once held as basic, fundamental truths about the world – beliefs that you just assumed were true and thus would never have considered questioning – that you now no longer hold or hold in a much more tentative manner. After we get past abandoned belief in Santa Claus and the Tooth Fairy and center on religious beliefs, I find that almost all of my students can identify what they once considered fundamental, obvious, non-negotiable beliefs about God's nature or relationship with the world that they have abandoned or modified. Few, I grant, have come to question belief in the existence of a personal supreme power of any sort. However, many now hold fundamentally different beliefs on such issues as the nature of God's power (whether God does or even can unilaterally control all earthly affairs), the nature of God's knowledge (whether God can foreknow that which we will freely do), the epistemic status of the Bible (whether it is in fact inerrant in every sense), and subjective immortality (whether there is an afterlife, what it will be like, and what is required of us to be in God's presence when we die).

Moreover, I do not think my students are unique in this respect. I believe that all (or almost all) religious exclusivists do in fact abandon or modify some beliefs that had previously functioned as their basic, non-negotiable assumptions about the nature of reality.

Furthermore, I do not think that the practical significance of rock bottom beliefs can be overemphasized. Even those basic beliefs about God's nature that might seem to some people very abstract and removed from everyday living can be shown to have practical implications for how believers live their lives. For instance, a believer's perspective on God's power and knowledge often dictates how she explains and responds to sickness and death.

The direct impact of other basic, rock bottom beliefs is even clearer. For instance, it still seems fundamentally (just obviously) true to many people world-wide that men have some sort of God-given, inherent authority over women, or that certain ethnic groups have God-given superiority, or that certain sexual orientations are perversions of God's ideal, or that humans have God-given authority over the rest of nature, or that God desires heretics to be silenced. And these fundamental religious beliefs, along with many more like them, clearly do affect how those who hold such beliefs relate to themselves and others.

Accordingly, it seems to me that all religious exclusivists should quite naturally find themselves asking (or at least feel some compulsion to ask)[22] the question I often find my students asking: given that I have abandoned or modified some beliefs once held as rock bottom (and will probably continue to do so in the future), and given that rock bottom beliefs have practical import, what can I do to help ensure that my current rock bottom beliefs are those that ought to be guiding my thoughts and actions?

This is a complex question. However, I find many of my students suggesting what I believe all religious exclusivists should acknowledge at this point: that one obvious way for a person to ensure the adequacy of her rock bottom beliefs is for her to submit such beliefs to focused belief assessment. In fact, given the main alternative of which I can conceive – to seek non-reflective affective reaffirmation of one's basic beliefs – I don't see how it can be denied that such assessment is the most reasonable way for the religious exclusivist who desires truth to ensure that her current rock bottom beliefs are those that ought to be guiding her behaviour.[23]

However, even if this is so, one important question remains unanswered: If we assume (I think properly) that not all rock bottom beliefs can be submitted to simultaneous belief assessment, how should such belief assessment proceed? One possibility, of course, is simply to submit each rock bottom belief in turn to assessment as time and energy allow. However, something else I've learned from my students is, I believe, instructive at this point.

When I ask my students to attempt to determine why they have abandoned or modified beliefs once held as rock bottom, the main reason cited is not that someone demonstrated to them that such beliefs were self-contradictory or incompatible with other beliefs held. Rather, the main reason cited is that upon discovering that seeming peers held different beliefs and then considering why this was so – upon entering into a comparative assessment of these conflicting beliefs – they either felt the need to abandon or modify, or, more frequently, simply found themselves abandoning or modifying, what had once just seemed true. In other words, it is usually because they 'voluntarily' did what Basinger's Rule asks of them when faced with peer conflict that they abandoned or modified what had functioned as rock bottom beliefs. Moreover, again I do not think that my students are unique in this respect.

Accordingly, to extrapolate, it seems to me we now find ourselves with a more plausible (and, I believe, more practical) response to the question of how the religious exclusivist should go about assessing her rock bottom religious beliefs. Given that belief modification does in fact often occur (I would say does most often occur) in the face of epistemic peer conflict, it seems to me quite reasonable for a religious exclusivist to determine that she should submit rock bottom beliefs to assessment whenever she comes to realize that they are beliefs on which seemingly sincere, equally knowledgeable individuals disagree.

To do so will not, as I have already acknowledged, resolve most, or even many, epistemic disputes in an objective manner. However, to the extent that religious exclusivists practice Basinger's Rule in the face of peer conflict, they can, I believe, have greater confidence that they are thinking and acting in ways they will not regret later. That is, they can have greater confidence that they are not thinking and acting in ways they would not have thought or acted had they consciously assessed the relevant foundational beliefs beforehand.

Or, to state this important point in a somewhat different manner, A.C. Ewing once argued in relation to ethical intuitions (ethical rock bottom beliefs) that although such beliefs are by definition not based on reason and observation, the most reliable of these intuitions are those that have been assessed using reason and observation.[24] The same is true, I believe, with respect to rock bottom religious beliefs. The 'best' (most reliable) rock bottom beliefs are those the exclusivist finds herself holding after such beliefs have been subjected to belief assessment.

I can envision, though, one more potential line of criticism. It may well be, it might be argued, that most religious exclusivists do over time modify or abandon what were once thought to be basic, foundational beliefs in their belief systems. However, it is wrong to claim that these beliefs actually were rock bottom beliefs. Real rock bottom religious beliefs are by their very nature non-falsifiable. That is, because of their actual status in the belief system, nothing is allowed (perhaps nothing can be allowed psychologically) to count against them, and no amount of assessment will change this fact. So while the basic, foundational beliefs abandoned or modified by exclusivists may indeed have previously been *unquestioned* beliefs that appeared to be rock bottom, the fact that they were abandoned or modified simply demonstrates that they really weren't rock bottom beliefs in the first place. And this in turn means that Gellman's claim that rock bottom beliefs are immune from assessment remains intact.

Not surprisingly, I deny that religious exclusivists do not in fact ever modify or abandon real rock bottom beliefs. However, even if it is true that exclusivists do not (because they cannot) assess real rock bottom beliefs, the following question remains: how is the exclusivist to know which of the fundamental, basic beliefs that 'just seem true' to her actually are real rock bottom beliefs and which aren't? And the only reasonable answer, I believe, is for the religious exclusivist to subject these beliefs to assessment, especially in the face of epistemic peer conflict. In short, even if it happens to be the case that real rock bottom beliefs are immune from change, the fact that the religious exclusivist has no *a priori* basis for determining which of her basic, foundational beliefs are actually rock bottom means that she still has good reason to practice Basinger's Rule.

Accordingly, we must conclude, I believe, that Gellman's appeal to rock bottom beliefs is not the decisive criticism of Basinger's Rule he believes it to be. Specifically, we must conclude that since rock bottom (basic) beliefs change over time and are of such tremendous significance, religious exclusivists who desire truth should, at the very least, recognize the value in doing more than simply defending their right to affirm such beliefs, as Gellman suggests. They should see that there are good reasons to assure themselves that those basic (rock bottom) religious beliefs that form the core of their exclusivity really are beliefs worthy of continued acceptance, especially in the face of epistemic peer conflict.[25]

Gellman's Additional Challenge

More recently, though, Gellman has offered a somewhat different challenge to my position.[26] While the critique we have been considering centers on the nature of the basic beliefs held by the exclusivist, his newer challenge centers on the degree of confidence the exclusivist has in her beliefs:

> [As] my grandmother used to say: 'If the wheel does not squeak, don't oil it'. Only a wheel that squeaks requires attention. So the epistemic strategy should be to let the beliefs that do not 'squeak' be the unreflective base for considering the beliefs that do 'squeak'. A belief, B, 'squeaks' when one's confidence in B is challenged (1) by others of one's beliefs more firmly held than B, or (2) by an epistemic tension between B and others of one's other beliefs held perhaps equally firmly, causing one to at least consider giving B up to restore epistemic peace, or (3) by a new belief-candidate that one perceives to threaten one's belief in B or its justification (including a belief-candidate to the effect that one's home group is not to be trusted.) As long as a person's home belief does not squeak for her, she will be rationally entitled to reflect on her other beliefs and on new belief-candidates by its lights, not having subjected it itself to reflective scrutiny.[27]

In other words, while Gellman now seems to acknowledge that the exclusivist may at times need to subject even her basic beliefs to assessment, he does still deny that the exclusivist needs always to engage in belief assessment in the face of epistemic peer conflict, as Basinger's Rule claims. It is *only*, he tells us, if such conflict challenges the exclusivist's confidence in her beliefs in certain stipulated ways that she needs to subject the affected beliefs to assessment, that is, attempt to adjudicate the conflict. Otherwise, she 'may rationally invoke her unreflective religious belief to defeat opposing religious claims, without having to consider the question any further'.[28] She may, in short, justifiably ignore Basinger's Rule.

Is it really true, though, that an exclusivist can justifiably retain the requisite confidence when challenged by those who appear to be equally knowledgeable and sincere? As Gellman sees it, there are at least two epistemic contexts in which it is perfectly rational for the exclusivist to retain such confidence in the face of seeming peer conflict.

First, we are told, an exclusivist does not simply affirm a set of propositions. Her beliefs form an interpretive framework through which 'she understands God, history, the nature of the self, human suffering, human cognition, values, the future, the afterlife, metaphysics, art, and, finally, other religions'. And as long as her interpretive framework 'provides her with all she rationally needs to interpret her world satisfactorily', she is justified in not losing confidence in the face of seeming peer conflict and thus justified in not attempting to adjudicate such conflict or even subjecting her own belief to any form of assessment. She can, rather, 'interpret the religious claims of [her epistemic challengers] in her own terms'.[29]

Second, as Gellman sees it, an exclusivist may well believe not only that God is the source of truth but that the key to truth is a proper relationship with God and that 'it would be a serious violation of her relationship to God for her to consider for a moment that some other religion might be true rather than the one God encourages her in daily'. And the exclusivist who holds this perspective on truth, we are told, is rationally justified in remaining confident in the face of peer challenge without submitting the beliefs in question to belief assessment.[30]

However, might not someone note here, Gellman correctly points out, that whether one is a Jew or Christian or Buddhist is mainly an accident of birth – a function of where one is born? And given this fact, does not each of us have 'an epistemic responsibility to reflect on his belief, and not leave it at the unreflective level'? That is, given this fact, does not Basinger's Rule still hold?

Gellman believes that for the confident exclusivist – the exclusivist who is experiencing no 'squeaking' – the answer is no. If a religious perspective were actually a function of place of birth, then belief assessment, he allows, might be required. However, Gellman argues, 'since a believer is rationally justified to start with what he is taught by his elders and since he is rationally justified not to oil the wheels of his religious beliefs if they don't squeak, he can be rationally justified in believing that his devotion to his home religion is no accident'.[31] That is, the confident exclusivist, Gellman believes, can justifiably deny that his religious perspective is actually a function of place of birth, and thus, concludes Gellman, that the obvious correlation between belief and place of birth makes belief assessment necessary.

I want first, in response, to question Gellman's implicit assumption that the religious exclusivist will, in fact, often find herself, even in the face of peer challenge, affirming basic beliefs that do not 'squeak'.

With respect to inter-system peer conflict – with respect to peer conflict between or among proponents of basic theistic systems such as Christianity, Islam and Judaism – I grant that this assumption is plausible. It is Gellman's contention, remember, that a belief 'squeaks' only when one's confidence in . this belief has been challenged by (1) an incompatible belief held more firmly, (2) an incompatible belief held equally firmly, or (3) a new belief-candidate that cannot easily be dismissed. However, (1) and (2) almost never apply to the competing claims of other basic theistic systems. And the conflicting claims of (the new belief-candidates offered by) other basic systems are almost never considered serious threats since an exclusivist's own basic theistic system almost always offers what are perceived as plausible reasons for believing the competing claims of other basic system(s) to be false. Moreover, to be fair to Gellman, it is only inter-system peer conflict with which he is concerned.

However, I believe that intra-system peer conflict – peer conflict within basic theistic systems – almost always produces 'squeaking'. Consider, for example, the current debates among seemingly sincere, knowledgeable Christians over the extent of God's power (whether God is all controlling or self-limiting) and the extent of God's knowledge (whether God knows infallibly future free choices). It has been my experience that since those on both sides claim allegiance to the same God and, more importantly, normally the same avenues of truth – what the Bible says, what the Spirit affirms, what other respected believers hold, etc. – it is very difficult for those on either side to dismiss easily the incompatible beliefs of their competitors. In fact, those on both sides often find such intra-system peer conflict so troubling that they are eager to see if some accommodation (synthesis) is possible.

Furthermore, the intra-system debates to which most exclusivists are exposed often directly or indirectly highlight for them possible consistency problems within their own belief systems. I have often found, for instance, that when students initially enter into discussions over the extent of God's power, many want boldly to maintain that God is in total control in the sense that nothing, especially human choice or behaviour, can keep God from bringing about that which he desires to accomplish. However, many of these same students also believe firmly that prayer changes things in the sense that whether God does or does not do that which he would like to do is dependent in part on whether we ask or fail to ask that he do so. When it is pointed out that this latter belief seems to presuppose that God has voluntarily given up control over some of what occurs (and that this in turn seems incompatible with their claim that God's activity is independent of human activity), the students in question quite often begin to feel uneasy, usually to the point where they believe it necessary to at least 'clarify' their position.

In short, as I see it, acknowledged intra-system peer conflict almost always challenges a theist's confidence.

However, even if this were not the case, I remain uneasy about Gellman's key contention: that we need only assess those beliefs in which we have lost confidence. Our own experience clearly shows us that we can, and do at times, lose confidence in beliefs in which we once had a great deal of confidence, and that this is frequently due to the fact that these beliefs were rationally assessed. Consequently, if, as I am assuming, our epistemic goal should be to maximize truth, then I just don't see how Gellman's 'if it doesn't squeak, don't oil it' maxim can be considered a serious challenge to my claim that the exclusivist faced with epistemic peer conflict ought to engage in belief assessment. At the very least, I don't see this maxim as a meaningful challenge to my claim that belief assessment is at least a very good idea for the exclusivist faced with such conflict.

I also remain uneasy about the two epistemic contexts in which Gellman believes it is rational for the exclusivist to retain confidence (and thus justifiably refrain from engaging in belief assessment) in the face of peer conflict. With respect to Gellman's first contention – that an exclusivist need not engage in belief assessment as long as she believes her interpretive framework provides her with all she rationally needs to interpret her world satisfactorily – I certainly agree, as already noted, that most exclusivists possess interpretive frameworks that can consistently accommodate all aspects of reality, including 'the claims of others'. And, as also noted, I believe that, ultimately, the proponent of a specific religious perspective is justified in affirming her perspective because she believes it best interprets reality as she experiences it. However, given that such interpretive frameworks are not only of tremendous practical significance but also change over time for most theists, it seems to me that the religious exclusivist who desires truth should recognize the value in doing more than simply defending her right to affirm her current interpretive framework. It seems to me, rather, that the exclusivist should, in the face of peer conflict, consider it at least a very good idea to engage in the type of belief assessment necessary to ensure that her current interpretive framework is indeed the one she wants to continue to allow to guide her thinking.

Gellman's second contention – that an exclusivist is justified in refraining from attempting to resolve peer conflict if she believes this might negatively affect her relationship with God, the source of truth – is more challenging since it does assume that truth is the goal. Moreover, it has been my experience that exclusivists often do appeal to this line of reasoning in response to challenges to their perspectives, especially when these challenges are from outside their own basic belief systems. That is, exclusivists often do refrain from a serious consideration of competing claims, especially those of other basic systems, because they fear that such assessment would weaken their relationship with God and thus lessen their ability to discover or retain the truth. But two difficulties resurface.

First, while it is true that exclusivists sometimes refrain from assessing firmly held beliefs in the face of intra-system challenge because of a fear that such assessment would have a negative effect on their personal relationship with God and, thus, on their search for truth, I know of no religious exclusivist who really believes that intra-system belief assessment should always, or even usually, be avoided – who really holds that it is always, or even usually, justifiable for an exclusivist to remain unreflective about her firmly held beliefs in the face of epistemic peer conflict within her system. In fact, as already mentioned, many faith traditions encourage, if not require, intra-system belief assessment. Christian exclusivists, for instance, believe it is important to 'study to show themselves approved' and to be ready to 'give a reason for their faith'. While, admittedly, the goal here is not at times to find the truth but rather to share it, at other times the goal clearly is to find or clarify God's truth in the face of ambiguity or challenge.[32]

Second, a point raised in relation to Plantinga again becomes relevant. If exclusivists believe it is rational to refrain from considering the incompatible claims of other religions for the reason in question, they run into a conceptual difficulty if they engage in proselytization – if they attempt to convert someone from another religion to their basic theistic systems. Specifically, they want the person they desire to 'convert' to consider seriously the claims being presented (in fact might even believe this person ought to do so) while at the same time also believing (per hypothesis) that it is perfectly rational for this person to refrain from considering seriously what they are saying if she believes that to do so could lead her away from truth. And this, as I see it, is no small problem. Gellman happens to come from a faith tradition that doesn't emphasize evangelism, but the majority of exclusivists come from traditions that do emphasize (or even require) that proponents attempt to convince others to 'see the light'.

These difficulties, as I see it, in no way challenge the claim that serious belief assessment can negatively influence a person's relationship with God. However, these difficulties are, I believe, sufficient to counter the claim that the exclusivist can justifiably refrain from belief assessment because she fears a negative impact upon her faith.

Conclusion

Let me in closing emphasize what I have and have not attempted to argue with respect to the key question with which this chapter is concerned: the question of what, if anything, the reality of epistemic peer conflict requires of the exclusivist.

I have not argued that epistemic peer conflict requires the exclusivist to refrain from the affirmation of exclusivistic beliefs. Nor have I argued that it is wrong for religious exclusivists to defend themselves against those who claim otherwise. However, some of the most influential religious exclusivists in philosophical circles – for instance, Plantinga and Gellman –

want to stop at that point. That is, as they see it, the only really important task of the exclusivist, in the face of epistemic peer conflict, is to defend her right to her exclusivity.

It is here that I believe they go wrong. Religious exclusivists need to recognize, I have argued, the value in doing more than simply defending their positions. They need to see that there are good reasons to assure themselves that those religious beliefs that form the core of their exclusivity really are beliefs worthy of continued acceptance, especially in the face of epistemic peer conflict.

Is such assessment an epistemic *obligation* for religious exclusivists? I remain convinced that the answer is yes. But what I have primarily attempted to defend in this chapter is a weaker, but still important, contention: that religious exclusivists should at the very least acknowledge that there are good reasons for them to 'voluntarily' do so.

Notes

1. For a comprehensive overview of such issues, see Michael Peterson, William Hasker, Bruce Reichenbach and David Basinger, *Reason and Religious Belief: An Introduction to the Philosophy of Religion*, 2nd edn. (New York: Oxford University Press, 1998).
2. Jerome I. Gellman, 'Epistemic Peer Conflict and Religious Beliefs: A Reply to Basinger', *Faith and Philosophy* 15 (April 1998), p. 231.
3. As noted in Chapter 1 (note 1), since most philosophers use 'religious diversity' to label the type of epistemic tension with which this book is concerned, I normally do so also. However, since this chapter is concerned primarily with Basinger's Rule and this principle is formally stated in terms of epistemic peer conflict, I will in this chapter retain this terminology.
4. To say that there exists no objective reason to doubt that our epistemic competitors are equally knowledgeable and sincere is not to say that we cannot believe (even justifiably) that they are not actually on equal epistemic footing. It is, rather, to say that we cannot demonstrate on grounds acceptable to all that they are not on equal footing. A fuller discussion of this important distinction occurs later in this chapter.
5. David Basinger, 'Plantinga, Pluralism and Justified Religious Belief', *Faith and Philosophy* 5 (October 1988), pp. 67–80.
6. See, for example, ibid., or David Basinger, 'Is Belief in God Rational?', *New Scholasticism* 60 (1986), pp. 163–85.
7. The reasons why I believe this to be the case are discussed in detail later in this chapter.
8. I am here talking about epistemic obligation – a 'should' of rationality. However, to the extent that we have a moral obligation to meet our epistemic obligations, for a person to choose not to submit one's beliefs to assessment in the face of epistemic peer conflict may well be a moral, as well as an epistemic, shortcoming.
9. For a more thorough discussion of this point, see David Basinger, *The Case For Freewill Theism* (Downers Grove, IL: InterVarsity Press, 1996), pp. 16–20.
10. Alvin Plantinga, 'Pluralism: A Defense of Exclusivism', in *The Philosophical Challenge of Religious Diversity*, Kevin Meeker and Philip L. Quinn, eds (New York: Oxford University Press, 2000), pp. 172–192. Jerome Gellman, 'Religious Diversity and the Epistemic Justification of Religious Belief', *Faith and Philosophy* 10 (July 1993), pp. 345–64; Gellman, 'Epistemic Peer Conflict and Religious Belief'.
11. Plantinga, 'Pluralism', p. 189.
12. Ibid., p. 190.
13. Alvin Plantinga, 'Ad Hick', *Faith and Philosophy* 14 (July 1997), p. 296
14. Ibid., p. 296.

15. Ibid., p. 296.
16. Ibid., p. 296. Plantinga, it should also be noted, believes that the proponents of other basic religious perspectives – for example, Islamic exclusivists – can use the same line of reasoning to claim justifiably that their competitors – for example, Christians – are not on equal epistemic footing.
17. Kelly Clarke offers an analogous line of reasoning in relation to transformational parity (see Clarke, 'Perils of Pluralism', *Faith and Philosophy* 14 (July 1997), p. 316). Specifically, he argues that while an exclusivist can never justifiably deny that there is actual transformational parity among diverse religious perspectives on the basis of personal experience, she can justifiably deny such parity if the denial follows from (or is required by) other beliefs within her perspective. I think Clarke is basically correct. In fact, I utilize his line of reasoning as support for my critique of John Hick in Chapter 4. But Clarke acknowledges not only that the proponent of no specific religious perspective can demonstrate on grounds that are (or should be) accepted by all rational people that her perspective is actually more successful at moral and spiritual transformation than are divergent perspectives, he argues that *any* exclusivist (the proponent of any of the incompatible religious perspectives) can justifiably deny transformational parity if such a denial follows from (or is required by) other justified beliefs within her perspective. So, clearly, it is also the case that his comments are not a threat to the type of epistemic parity found in Basinger's Rule.
18. For a detailed description of these positions, see Basinger, *The Case for Freewill Theism*, pp. 21–37.
19. What Plantinga offers here is not just a possible theoretical response to religious epistemic peer conflict. I have taught thousands of sincere Christians from over 30 denominations over the past 27 years and have frequently witnessed versions of this same line of reasoning used by students to justify their claim that those with whom they disagree are not true epistemic peers.
20. Some of the material in this section on Plantinga first appeared (in significantly different form) in 'The Challenge of Religious Diversity: A Middle Ground', *Sophia* 38/1 (March–April, 1999), pp. 41–53. Used with permission.
21. Gellman, 'Religious Diversity and the Epistemic Justification of Religious Belief', p. 354.
22. I add this parenthetical phrase because it seems to me that the significance of our rock bottom beliefs obligates us, in principle, to subject them to belief assessment. For someone to say that she simply does not feel she wants to submit her beliefs to assessment would, as I see it, not be justified.
23. Some religious exclusivists might dispute this claim, arguing instead for the superiority of some non-reflective means of belief assessment – for example, direct divine guidance. But most religious exclusivists, including all those mentioned in this paper, believe that beliefs are properly subject to rational assessment. And for such exclusivists it seems to me clear that focused belief assessment is the best way to ensure a satisfactory set of rock bottom (basic) beliefs.

It is also crucial that we remember that the sort of assessment encouraged by Basinger's Rule does not require that the exclusivist produce objective 'proof' for her perspective before she can continue to affirm this perspective justifiably. She can justifiably retain belief as long as it appears to her, for any number of subjective reasons, that her perspective is superior (her rock bottom beliefs are in fact true).
24. A.C. Ewing, 'Ethical Intuitionism', in Robert E. Dewey and Robert H. Hurlbutt, eds, *An Introduction to Ethics* (Macmillan, 1977), pp. 161–5.
25. Again, it is important to emphasize that what is being asked of the exclusivist is not that she demonstrate in some objective fashion that her perspective is superior. What is being asked is that she assure herself that she actually does have what she believes to be sufficient reasons to continue to affirm her perspective.

Some of the material in this section on Gellman first appeared (in slightly different form) in 'Religious Diversity: Where Exclusivists Often Go Wrong', *International Journal for the Philosophy of Religion* 47 (2000), pp. 43–55. Used by permission.

26. Jerome Gellman, 'In Defense of Contented Religious Exclusivism', *Religious Studies* 36 (December 2000), pp. 401–17.
27. Ibid., p. 403.
28. Ibid., p. 403.
29. Ibid., p. 404.
30. Ibid., p. 405.
31. Ibid., p. 407.
32. It should be noted again that Gellman is discussing inter-system peer conflict, so he may agree that this second condition does not hold at the intra-system level.

Chapter 3

Diversity and Justified Belief

In Chapter 2, I argued that the religious exclusivist has good reason – if not an obligation – to assess her beliefs in the face of diversity (epistemic peer conflict)[1]. Not everyone, as we have seen, agrees that this is so. However, most philosophers agree on one point: that such assessment will not normally resolve peer conflict in an objective manner. That is, most agree that while the consideration of criteria such as self-consistency and comprehensiveness can rule out certain options, there exists no set of criteria that will allow us to resolve most cases of religious epistemic disputes in a neutral, non-question-begging manner.[2]

In this chapter, I want to discuss what follows if this is correct. If, in fact, belief assessment will not normally result in an objective adjudication of the competing claims, then in what epistemic position does this leave the exclusivist? Specifically, can she then justifiably retain her exclusivistic belief?

A number of prominent philosophers of religion have shared perspectives on this question. I will in this chapter outline the thoughts of four – William Alston, J.L. Schellenberg, William Wainwright and Philip Quinn – also sharing in each case what I see to be the strengths and weaknesses of the position *vis-à-vis* my own.[3]

William Alston

As Alston sees it, the *prima facie* challenge that epistemic peer conflict poses for the exclusivist is the following. Seemingly knowledgeable, sincere people affirm religious beliefs systems that are clearly incompatible in some ways. Moreover, proponents of each system have sufficient internal reasons to believe they are right – for example, proponents of each can justifiably maintain that their systems are self-consistent, have an explanation for the existence of incompatible systems, and transform people in the manner predicted. However, at best, proponents of only one of these systems can actually be right, and there exist no external, neutral, non-question-begging grounds by which it can be determined objectively who is correct. While this alone doesn't give us a justifiable basis for maintaining that the proponent of any given system is wrong, it does give us a sufficient reason to deny that the proponent of any specific system – for example, Christianity or Buddhism or Islam or Judaism – can justifiably (rationally) maintain that her system is the truth. That is, because the proponents of none of the incompatible theistic belief systems have a non-question-begging basis (have a stronger objective basis than proponents of any other system)

31

for claiming they have the truth, we do have good reason to conclude that a theist is 'arbitrary in picking [her perspective] as the one that is sufficiently reliable for rational acceptance', and thus to conclude that no theist can justifiably continue to be an exclusivist.[4]

Alston takes this challenge seriously. He disagrees with those who argue that, despite appearances, there exist no serious epistemic peer conflicts among basic theistic systems. Such conflicts, he believes, are real and significant. Moreover, since he assumes a realist theory of truth, he also agrees that, whether or not we have any way of deciding the matter, at best only one of the basic systems can be correct.[5]

Even more importantly, Alston acknowledges that the reality of epistemic peer conflict – the fact that knowledgeable people affirm incompatible religious belief systems – should, for the proponent of any given belief system, diminish her confidence in the superiority of this particular system (her confidence that her system contains *the* truth). Accordingly, he recommends that the exclusivist 'do whatever seems feasible to search for common ground on which to adjudicate the crucial differences between the world religions, seeking a way to show in a non-circular way which of the contenders is correct'.[6] In short, he affirms a version of Basinger's Rule.

However, Alston assumes (and it appears actually believes) that there exists *at present* no such common ground – that we do not possess objective, non-question-begging criteria by which we can settle the issue. So the key question for Alston becomes the following: is it true, as the critic concludes, that since there exists no objective, non-question-begging basis for determining which basic theistic system contains the truth, the proponent of no specific system can justifiably (rationally) continue to maintain that her system is superior – can justifiably remain an exclusivist?

Alston's response is based on what he sees as a crucial distinction between two types of epistemic contexts. There exist epistemic contexts, he tells us, in which 'it is clear what would constitute non-circular grounds for supposing one of the contestants to be superior to the others, even if we don't have such grounds'. That is, there are contexts in which 'we know what would decisively show that one account is the correct one' – in which there is a commonly accepted 'procedure for settling disputes'. For example, Alston points out, if two witnesses to an automobile accident have different recollections of what occurred, then even if we cannot determine objectively which, if either, is correct, we do in this case know what would decisively decide the issue – for instance, a home video of the incident, or evidence to the end that one of the two witnesses is a habitual liar. Thus there is at least the live possibility of settling the issue. And, consequently, in such cases, he acknowledges, it isn't (or at least may well not be) rational for a person to continue to maintain that her position is superior.[7]

Or, to state this important point somewhat differently, it is Alston's contention that when individuals acknowledge the existence of a common objective ground for adjudicating an epistemic dispute between them, but cannot, given these grounds, agree on a clear winner, then none of the disputants can justifiably claim that her perspective is in fact superior.

However, in the case of epistemic conflict among proponents of basic theistic systems (basic world religions), there exists, Alston believes, no such common ground for settling such disputes. That is, it is his belief that 'since, as we are assuming, each of the major world religions involves (at least one) distinct [basic belief system], with its own way of going from experiential input to beliefs formulated in terms of that scheme, and its own system of overriders, the competitors lack the kind of common procedure for settling disputes that is available to participants in a shared [basic belief system]' .[8]

Moreover, this 'lack of common ground', Alston holds, 'alters drastically the epistemic bearings of an unresolved incompatibility'. It still remains true, he grants, that the reality of epistemic peer conflict diminishes justification. But the fact that 'we are at a loss to specify what such [common ground] would look like' means, he argues, that with respect to those basic theistic belief systems that are self-consistent and efficacious, it is not 'irrational for one to remain an exclusivist' – not irrational for the proponent of any of these basic belief systems to continue to hold that the system to which she is presently committed contains the truth.[9] That is, as Alston sees it, given the absence of common ground, the proponent of any given internally validated basic theistic belief system can 'justifiably engage in his/her own [belief system] despite not being able to show that it is epistemically superior to the competition'.[10]

In fact, at one point he goes even further. Because there exists at present no neutral ground for adjudicating epistemic conflicts among basic theistic systems, it is not only the case, Alston argues, that an exclusivist is justified (rational) in continuing to consider her own perspective superior. Since we do not even know what a non-circular reason for demonstrating the superiority of any of these systems would look like, the 'only rational course' for an exclusivist 'is to sit tight' with the belief system 'which has served so well in guiding [her] activity in the world'. In other words, as Alston understands it, given the absence of common ground for adjudicating inter-system disputes, it is not rational for a person to stop being the exclusivist she is – to stop maintaining that her system is superior.[11]

I, of course, agree with Alston's contention that epistemic peer conflict poses a problem that requires an attempt to find common ground for resolution, since to grant that this is so is simply to affirm a version of Basinger's Rule. However, I am troubled by the distinction Alston attempts to draw between inter-system and intra-system epistemic peer conflict. Specifically, it seems to me that Alston is wrong to argue that with respect to intra-system conflicts, we know how to go about settling them, even if we can't actually do so in a given case, while with respect to inter-system conflicts we have no such common ground.

First, Alston's claim that we have no neutral, non-question-begging criteria – no common ground – for adjudicating the inter-system disputes in question strikes me as, at best, ambiguous. He can't really mean that there exists absolutely no common ground for attempted resolution since he himself limits his discussion of basic theistic systems to those that are self-consistent and efficacious. Moreover, proponents of almost all basic theistic systems grant that these two conditions, plus comprehensiveness (accounting for all the relevant data), are necessary criteria for justified belief. In short, it seems to me that even Alston does (or should) agree that there exists a recognized set of objective criteria for adjudicating inter-system peer conflict.

I grant that these criteria will not allow for the objective resolution of such conflict (are not sufficient to resolve these disputes objectively) and also grant that we are not in a position to even say what else could be done. However, to say that we have no agreement on a set of *sufficient* objective criteria for conflict resolution (which is what I think Alston really wants to argue) is very different than saying that we have no agreement on *necessary* objective criteria for doing so (which is how Alston can easily be read).

I am most troubled, though, by Alston's characterization of the nature of intra-system peer conflict. Alston is certainly correct in pointing out that disputants in inter-system debates do normally have access to objective adjudicatory criteria. Within Christianity, for instance, there continue to be epistemic disputes over the nature of God's power, knowledge and goodness. However, even though objective criteria for conflict resolution do exist within most basic theistic systems, an appeal to such criteria seldom settles the disputes in question. For example, within Christianity, there do exist explicit criteria for the adjudication of peer conflict. Specifically, the disputants in conflicts concerning the nature of God's power or knowledge or goodness often do agree that the right answer is what the Bible says and/or what tradition tells us and/or what the Spirit of God confirms. But there is, in fact, almost never agreement on which perspective these criteria support. Or, to put the point differently, the participants agree on the objective criteria that would resolve the conflict, but they disagree on what these criteria establish. Nor do I know of any non-question-begging way of furthering such discussions. In fact, I cannot envisage how we could even go about trying to find sufficient objective criteria (sufficient common ground) for the resolution of such issues.

Accordingly, since these are the very same characteristics Alston ascribes to inter-system peer conflict, we must conclude, I believe, that inter-system and intra-system conflict are on equal epistemic footing. In both cases, there are some common objective adjudicatory criteria to which we can appeal (although more within systems than among them), and in both cases the criteria are not sufficient for the objective adjudication of most significant differences. In other words, in both cases, we have adjudicatory criteria all consider necessary; in neither case do we have adjudicatory criteria all consider sufficient. So I believe that whatever we decide about the relevance of common ground for justified belief must apply equally to epistemic peer conflict of both types.[12]

In fact, it seems to me that Alston ought to agree with me on this point. The key to his position on inter-system conflict is not that we have absolutely no common ground for adjudicating disputes at the inter-system level since, as I have argued, I think he implicitly grants that there do exist some necessary objective criteria for this purpose. The key to his position on inter-system conflict is his belief that we quickly exhaust what common ground we have and don't even see how we can go any further in a non-question-begging manner. Yet I think that he could, and should, acknowledge that this is exactly the situation we normally find ourselves in with respect to intra-system peer conflict as well.

However, whether or not I am right in claiming that both types of conflict are on equal epistemic footing, I think that Alston's contention – that when we have no way of even knowing what would count as criteria for objectively resolving an epistemic dispute in a non-question-begging manner, the only rational thing for each disputant to do is to sit tight with what she has – is simply too strong.

Let us first assume that I am right in maintaining that this claim should also apply to intra-system peer conflict and consider, for instance, the current intra-Christianity dispute over whether God has exhaustive knowledge of what individuals will freely do in the future. Given that this dispute centers on differing interpretations of what the accepted criteria for adjudication establish – differing understandings of what, for example, the Bible or the Spirit says on this issue – and given that we can at present conceive of no additional criteria acceptable to all that will allow us to settle the issue objectively, disputants would, given Alston's position, be irrational to change perspectives or even to suspend judgment.

Or let us assume that Alston's claim should be applied only to inter-system peer conflict – for example, to the inter-system dispute among Christians, Muslims, Jews, Buddhists and Hindu about the true nature of the Divine. Since there exists, in principle, no common ground for adjudicating this dispute, then the only rational course, given Alston's position, is for the disputants to sit tight with what they have.

However, in both cases, this conclusion seems to me incorrect. I certainly agree with Alston's weaker principle: that in such cases each disputant remains justified in retaining her current position. In other words, I think Alston is correct to argue that, if there exist no common criteria for settling the issue conclusively, a disputant *can* justifiably sit tight. But I see no reason – and Alston offers us none that I can find – why it would be wrong not to do so.

He might believe, or at least it might be argued, that the very fact that we have (per hypothesis) no objective reason to switch is itself a reason not to switch. However, to argue in this fashion seems to me to be based on a misunderstanding of the manner in which justifiable religious belief modification actually occurs. As I see it, most individuals do not modify religious beliefs because they feel compelled to do so by the force of the objective evidence. For instance, while it is sometimes true that a disputant in a debate over some aspect of religious doctrine will change or modify belief based on an interpretation of Scripture acceptable to all, this is not the way belief modification in the face of diversity normally occurs. That is, if one of the disputants changes or modifies belief in the face of conflict, it is not usually because the evidence has forced her to acknowledge that she could no longer justifiably retain her position. It is because she has considered the other person's position (the other person's interpretation of the data) and has come to see (or more accurately come to 'feel') over time that her opponent's perspective is superior, or that the issue is too ambiguous to hold a position firmly. This seems to me, for instance, to be what almost always happens when individuals switch basic theistic allegiances. And I can't see why such a change should be considered irrational, in either an intra-system or inter-system context.[13]

So I stand by my contention that Alston's stronger claim – that exclusivists ought to sit tight in the face of peer conflict – should be rejected. But, again, I am in strong agreement with his weaker claim: that proponents of a specific religious perspective (at both the intra-system and inter-system level, I would add) are justified in retaining their exclusivity in the face of peer conflict.[14]

J.L. Schellenberg

One of the philosophers highly critical of Alston's perspective on the epistemic status of the exclusivist is J.L. Schellenberg. The key to Alston's position, Schellenberg rightly notes, is his claim that in those cases of epistemic conflict in which we do not even know what would constitute independent, non-question-begging grounds for favoring one side, proponents of both sides are justified in continuing to maintain that their perspectives are correct. However, Schellenberg argues,

1. Necessarily, for any person S and any proposition p, S is justified in believing p only if, for any proposition q known by S to be entailed by p, S has justification for believing q.
2. Participants in the various religious experiential belief-forming practices, insofar as they are aware of the problem of religious diversity, know the denials of many other reliability claims to be entailed by their own.
3. For each such participant, continued belief in the reliability of her own practice is justified only if she has justification for a denial of the others' claims (from (1) and (2)).
4. Each lacks justification of the latter sort.
5. Hence each lacks justification of the former sort (from (3) and (4)).[15]

Or, stated in more informal terms, Schellenberg's complaint is essentially the following. When the competing claims in a religious epistemic conflict are incompatible, only one at most can be true. Moreover, since it is a necessary truth that a disputant in such a conflict is justified in continuing to maintain that her perspective is true only if she possesses non-question-begging justification for believing any proposition that is an entailment of this perspective, and since the truth of her perspective entails that any incompatible perspective is false, a disputant remains justified in continuing to maintain that her perspective is true only if she possesses non-question-begging justification for believing the incompatible perspective of any competitor to be false. However, since no disputant in religious conflicts possesses such justification, no disputant can be justified – as Alston incorrectly believes – 'in holding her own claim to be true'.[16] Or, as Schellenberg states this conclusion in another context, we must conclude that in the absence of objective, non-question-begging justification, none of the disputants in religious conflicts 'has justification for supposing the others' claims false'.[17]

However, isn't the general principle in play here – that we aren't justified in claiming that our perspective is true unless we can justifiably reject incompatible perspectives on non-question-begging grounds – simply too strong? For instance, since we cannot produce non-question-begging justification for the belief that we are not programmed 'brains in vats' on some distant planet, doesn't this mean that we are not justified in believing 'in the deliverances of the senses'?[18]

Schellenberg recognizes this sceptical implication of his position, so he makes a distinction between cases of conflict in which both sides offer (or at least possess) reasons for believing their perspectives to be true and those cases in which the basis for one side is only that we lack an objective reason to deny that it is true. In the latter case, such as in the hypothetical dispute between those who trust their senses and those who claim we could be 'brains in vats', since only those who trust their senses have positive reasons for believing their perspective to be true, they can appeal, he argues, to such reasons as non-question-begging justification for rejecting the other perspective and thus maintaining that their position is superior. But in cases where those on both sides have positive reasons for holding their positions, as is the case with respect to religious epistemic conflicts, it remains true, he claims, that a lack of non-question-begging grounds for rejecting an opponent's perspective renders belief in the superiority of one's own perspective unjustified.[19]

However, even here, difficulties remain. If Schellenberg is correct, then there exist many significant contexts in which epistemic justification is lacking. For example, as Philip Quinn and Kevin Meeker point out, there appears to be no non-question-begging way to settle the dispute between indeterminists and compatibilists.[20] Nor does there appear to be any non-question-begging way of resolving differences between those who think we do possess some sort of immaterial 'mind' and those who don't; or between those who believe that life begins at conception and those who don't; or those who believe that one race or gender has inherent authority and those who don't. Rather, in all such cases the disputants can offer reasons for their positions that cannot be countered in a totally non-question-begging manner. But do we really want to maintain, as we must, given Schellenberg's line of reasoning, that none of the disputants in such conflicts can therefore justifiably claim that she is correct – can claim that her position is the truth?

I, for one, do not. I am willing to grant for the sake of argument that 'necessarily, for any person S and any proposition p, S is justified in believing p only if, for any proposition q known by S to be entailed by p, S has justification for believing q'. That is, I am willing to grant that to the extent that a participant in an epistemic dispute is aware of claims incompatible with her own, continued belief in the superiority of her own perspective is justified only if she has justification for a denial of these claims. I'm also willing to grant (again) that there are many cases in which peer conflict cannot be settled objectively by an appeal to criteria accepted by all parties involved. That is, I'm even willing to grant that the reasons disputants have at their disposal are almost always clearly inadequate to establish objectively that the conflicting claims of their competitors are wrong.

However, it does not necessarily follow from any of this that the disputants in question have no justification for believing their competitors wrong, as Schellenberg believes. This conclusion follows only if we make the further assumption that a disputant can be justified in believing that her competitor's claims are false, and thus that hers are true, only if she can demonstrate this to be so by some non-question-begging line of reasoning – on the basis of some set of objective criteria accepted by all.

Why, though, ought we to accept this further assumption? It is certainly not a self-evident truth, nor is it an assumption widely accepted in philosophical circles today. Such an assumption, rather, is simply a variant of strong rationalism, the once popular epistemic claim that in order for a belief to be rationally accepted, it must be true in a way that should be convincing to any reasonable person. And strong rationalism is coming under increasing criticism.[21] Nor can I conceive of any non-question-begging basis on which Schellenberg could argue that the disputant in an epistemic conflict must produce non-question-begging evidence against the perspectives of her competitors before she can justifiably claim that her perspective is true. At the very least, no such argument appears in his discussion.

So I remain unconvinced. Schellenberg is entitled to his opinion. However, his basic assumption about what counts as adequate justification for claiming that an epistemic competitor's beliefs are false need not be granted. So I see no non-question-begging reason why those who attempt unsuccessfully to resolve epistemic peer conflict on the basis of common ground cannot, as Alston and I claim, justifiably continue to maintain that they are correct (and thus that their opponents are not) simply because their own subjective reasons seem to them most convincing. In fact, rather ironically, if the dispute over the basic justificatory principle under discussion is itself, as I believe, not subject to non-question-begging objective resolution, then, given Schellenberg's own argument, he is not justified in claiming that his interpretation is correct. Thus the force of his argument against Alston and me also for that reason collapses.

William Wainwright

William Wainwright agrees with Alston that the reality of epistemic peer conflict rightly diminishes confidence in a person's belief that her exclusivistic religious perspective is the correct one. But he is dissatisfied with Alston's contention that the 'facts of religious diversity do not suffice to override the positive considerations on the other side (the presumptive reliability of any socially established [belief practice], plus the internal self-support involved) to such an extent as to show that the practice lacks a degree of reliability appropriate to rational acceptance'.[22]

Wainwright first comments on an important category of individuals not yet explicitly addressed in our discussion: those 'epistemic observers' who are not committed to any of the perspectives in a religious dispute. Specifically, if we assume that there is no non-question-begging basis for adjudicating objectively between competing perspectives, and thus that the only support for the superiority of any given perspective comes from within (comes from the fact that the system works in practice and/or offers the most plausible interpretation of reality for its proponents), how ought the person not committed to any of the perspectives in question respond?[23]

As Wainwright sees it, since in this case the reasons for affirming any given perspective are also reasons against affirming all other incompatible perspectives, the outside observer has 'a rather decisive reason for suspending judgement' – 'for withholding assent altogether'.[24] But this seems to me a little strong. I agree that the absence of objective, non-question-begging common ground for adjudicating epistemic conflict allows the uncommitted observer justifiably to suspend judgement. However, it seems to me too strong to imply (if this is indeed what Wainwright means to imply) that this is the most rational choice.

Consider, for instance, the religiously uncommitted person who starts to consider seriously the Christian and Islamic perspectives. The fact that variations of these theistic systems are incompatible and that there exists no non-question-begging way to adjudicate this conflict should certainly be a significant consideration. In fact, such incompatibility would, I think, be a justifiable reason for someone not to make a personal commitment to either. I will even grant that if an uncommitted individual comparing these systems personally found both systems to be equally plausible or compelling, then perhaps a commitment to either one would be epistemically suspect. However, for someone to admit that there exist no objective means of establishing which system, if either, is the truth doesn't require that this person herself find both systems equally plausible or compelling.

Accordingly, if, after comparing the ways in which each side organizes and interprets reality, a previously uncommitted person makes a commitment to one or the other, I fail to see why this should in any way be considered less rational than remaining uncommitted. In fact, if, as I maintain, one need not have 'objective proof' for justified belief, then to the extent that a formerly uncommitted person finds one or the other much more plausible, or even unavoidably compelling, it seems to me perfectly reasonable for her to commit to this perspective.

What, though, of those who are already committed to a religious perspective? Specifically, is it epistemically rational for someone to remain an exclusivist – to continue to hold her perspective to be the truth – in the face of peer conflict that is not subject to objective, neutral resolution?

As Wainwright sees it, while it is 'epistemically rational to engage in a doxastic practice if there are good reasons for regarding it as reliable', it is 'epistemically irrational to engage in it if there are good reasons for thinking it unreliable'.[25] And while he grants (in his discussion of Alston) that the fact that Christianity (or Islam or Buddhism) is socially established, significantly self-supporting, and can't be shown objectively to be an unreliable source of true belief is a good reason to consider this basic doxastic system reliable, he also believes that the 'the *prima facie* reliability of incompatible mystical practices is a good reason for thinking that [any specific doxastic practice] is *prima facie* unreliable'.[26]

So where does this leave us? As Wainwright sees it, this depends on the extent to which we think unresolved peer conflict impacts rational belief, which, he grants, is difficult to determine since he acknowledges, with Alston, that we lack 'the conceptual resources to quantify degrees of rationality'.[27] However, his personal conviction is the following. Since it is doubtful that the reality of unresolved conflict outweighs the reasons for engaging in a specific practice, it is doubtful that we are in a position to say that engaging in a specific practice is irrational. On the other hand, if it really is the case that the metaphysical and empirical arguments for any specific theistic system – for example, Christianity or Islam or Buddhism – are no better than those supporting its rivals, then it is doubtful that we are in a position to say that the reasons for engaging in any one of these specific doxastic practices outweigh the problem of unresolved peer conflict to the extent that engaging in one of these practices remains rational.

It might be tempting, accordingly, Wainwright continues, to say as we often do in analogous situations in science that the most reasonable reaction is ' "acceptance" rather than "belief" '. That is, it might be tempting to say that while it is reasonable for a religious exclusivist to continue to engage in her practice in the sense that she continues to act as if it were true, 'it isn't clear that it is reasonable [for her] to believe it'.[28]

However, Wainwright points out, to be a proponent of a specific religious system is essentially to believe that the claims (at least the basic claims) of this system are true. Thus, for the religious exclusivist, any hard distinction between acting as if a set of religious beliefs were true and actually believing that they are true must be rejected. He does think, though, that it is legitimate for an exclusivist to consider, at times, whether there are independent (objective) reasons for or against the rationality of her commitment to the superiority of her belief system. Moreover, he adds,

A person who does this might (without making any obvious errors) come to the conclusion that although it is pragmatically rational to engage in the practice, it isn't epistemically reasonable to do so. If the pragmatic reasons are strong enough, he might further conclude he should suppress any doubts he may have and continue to engage in the practice, or that he should try, as it were, to live on two planes of consciousness at once – engaging in the practice on one level and hence trusting in its reliability while, on another, doubting it.[29]

And this, he concludes, may be a reasonable position for a proponent of a specific religious perspective to adopt in the face of epistemic peer conflict.

In summary, then, as I understand Wainwright, he believes that it is not epistemically irrational, and might be pragmatically rational, to continue to engage in a specific religious practice, given the reality of unresolved peer conflict. But he doubts that without metaphysical and empirical argumentation that forms 'a persuasive cumulative case argument for [a specific theistic practice]' commitment to a specific religious practice can be fully rational.[30]

I want first to comment on Wainwright's distinction between pragmatic and epistemic rationality. Specifically, I want to comment on his contention that while it may not be epistemically reasonable for the exclusivist to retain commitment to a specific theistic system in the face of unresolved conflict, it may be pragmatically reasonable to do so. It may be reasonable for an exclusivist to live as if her system is true while acknowledging that she no longer has sufficient independent (objective) reasons for believing it to be superior to other systems.

If Wainwright were saying simply that a person might decide (even justifiably) for pragmatic reasons to engage in certain doxastic practices (act as if a given theistic system is true) even though she no longer has sufficient reason to believe the system in question to be true, his claim would be relatively non-controversial. It is easy to stipulate any number of pragmatic reasons why someone might consider it best to continue to engage in the behaviours associated with a given theistic practice even though she has concluded that there isn't sufficient reason to believe this system is in fact true or superior to others. She might, for instance, do so in order not to disappoint friends or family, or to retain the benefit of interaction with others in the relevant faith community, or to avoid the guilt or embarrassment that might result if 'the faith' were abandoned.

However, Wainwright's rejection of any hard distinction between acting as if a belief is true and actually believing that it is true makes it clear that he has more in mind. His contention that a person might 'try, as it were, to live on two planes of consciousness at once – engaging in the practice on one level and hence trusting in its reliability while, on another, doubting it', shows that he thinks it may be justifiable for pragmatic reasons for an exclusivist to attempt to suppress her epistemic doubts to the point where she is continuing to engage in her religious practice because she believes at some level that the practice in question is actually reliable.

If this is what Wainwright means to say, then it seems to me that he is in one sense correct. There are situations, I believe, in which an exclusivist can justifiably attempt to suppress doubt to the point where she can continue to engage in her religious practice (affirm her religious perspective) with epistemic integrity. However, such cases, I will attempt to show, are of little value to Wainwright.

My argument to this end requires the distinction between two forms of doubt that can come into play in this context: affective doubt and epistemic doubt. To have affective doubt, as I will define it, is to have less personal conviction or confidence than one did previously that one's perspective is superior. It is to find oneself feeling less certain that something is true than one did before. To have epistemic doubt, as I will define it, is to question whether the reasons why one accepts a belief as true or superior are still sufficient.

To help sort out what I see as the relevant relationship between these two forms of doubt, let us consider the case of a young woman, Sue, who has been asked by her boyfriend, Bill, to trust in his love – to believe that she alone is his romantic interest – but who soon after receiving his pledge of love sees him frequently talking to another girl, sees the two of them smiling at each other in that 'certain way', finds that his phone is often engaged when she calls, finds that he has less time to spend with her than he formerly did, etc. In a case like this, it may well be that epistemic doubt will in fact lead to affective doubt. That is, it may well be that Sue will start to question whether her reasons for accepting Bill's claim of exclusive love are sufficient and for this reason begin to feel less certain that his claim is true. However, this may well not occur. It is also possible that Sue will for a time, or even indefinitely, continue to experience little or no affective doubt, even if she acknowledges that she now has no sufficient reason to believe his claim to be true.

On the other hand, even if we assume that Bill has not engaged in any such questionable behaviour, and thus that Sue has no objective basis for epistemic doubt, it could well be that she will find herself at some point with significant affective doubt – with much less confidence in Bill's love for her than she once had.

The same, I believe, is true with respect to religious belief. Epistemic doubt – less confidence in the sufficiency of one's reasons for belief – can lead to affective doubt – less personal conviction that what one believes is true. However, this need not be the case. It is possible to experience significant reduction of personal conviction in the truth of a religious belief in the total absence of epistemic doubt.

With this distinction in mind, it seems to me that we can construct a plausible scenario in which an exclusivist can justifiably attempt to suppress doubt for pragmatic reasons. Let us assume, for instance, that after serious consideration of the reasons for and against the rationality of continuing to affirm her current belief system in the face of epistemic peer conflict (perhaps, for instance, as a result of reading Gellman or Plantinga), an exclusivist comes to believe that such conflict poses little, if any, epistemic challenge to continued belief. But further suppose that she in fact finds that such conflict has diminished her personal confidence in the superiority of her system to the point that she honestly doubts (affectively) that her system contains more truth than other systems. In this case, it may well be reasonable for her to attempt to suppress her affective doubt to the point where she is continuing to engage in her religious practice because she believes it to be reliable. She might do so, for instance, in the hope that her 'feelings' will at some point come in line with her reason.

However, a scenario of this type is not open to Wainwright. I have just outlined a case in which someone believes epistemically that her system is superior, while no longer believing affectively (with much personal conviction) that this is so. Wainwright clearly wants us to consider a situation in which just the opposite is true: a situation in which a person believes (or at least desires to believe) affectively that her system is superior, but no longer believes epistemically that this is a rational position. And I doubt that, in situations of this sort, to attempt to suppress doubt for pragmatic reasons can be considered reasonable.

Returning again to our illustrative scenario, let us assume that Sue is now at the point where she has admitted to herself that she no longer has sufficient reason to believe that her boyfriend, Bill, really does love her only, although she still feels at some level that this is so. We could, in this case, easily understand why she might, for pragmatic reasons, want to suppress any doubt. She may, for instance, love him to the extent that she cannot conceive of life without him.

However, it seems to me that, in general, we have an epistemic duty not to attempt to keep that which we really believe to be true from affecting the way we behave, since to do so is incompatible with what I hold to be a primary tenet of rational behaviour: that we act in accordance with our most informed beliefs. And if this is so, then since to choose consciously not to fulfill an epistemic obligation is to forfeit epistemically rational (justified) belief, if Sue chooses consciously for pragmatic reasons to attempt to suppress her well-founded epistemic doubt, she has forfeited epistemic rationality.[31]

The same, I believe, holds for the religious exclusivist. We can understand why an exclusivist who comes to believe that there really aren't sufficient objective reasons for her to believe her religious perspective to be superior might want, for pragmatic reasons, to suppress this epistemic doubt. For instance, she might not be able to envision life without the guiding interpretive framework her religious perspective has supplied.[32] However, we have an epistemic duty, I am claiming, not to attempt to keep the 'truth' from affecting our behaviour. Accordingly, while it may be that an exclusivist can justifiably admit that her exclusivistic perspective is no longer rational but continue to live as if it is true for pragmatic reasons or because she can do nothing else, it cannot, as I see it, be considered epistemically reasonable (justifiable) for her to *choose* to suppress the very well-founded epistemic doubt in question.

In short, I don't believe that the sort of pragmatic behavior in question – to attempt to suppress one's epistemic doubt to the point that one believes at some level that the theistic perspective in question is true – is a viable option in this context and thus feel that Wainwright is too generous in allowing this as a reasonable alternative for the exclusivist.

Even more importantly, though, since I have already argued that a person can be fully rational in affirming her exclusivistic perspective, even in the face of acknowledged religious peer conflict, I obviously disagree with Wainwright's contention that without metaphysical and empirical argumentation that forms 'a persuasive cumulative case argument', the best that can probably be said about commitment to a specific theistic system is that it is not epistemically irrational.

I agree with Wainwright's contention that the reality of diversity does count against any given theistic perspective and thus that the exclusivist does need counterbalancing reasons to retain justified belief. And I agree that one of the reasons not available to the exclusivist is that objective argumentation establishes the superiority of her perspective. However, again I think that Wainwright makes too much of this lack of objective superiority in his weighting process.

As noted earlier, for a person to admit that there exists no *objective* basis for adjudicating between conflicting perspectives leaves open the question of how convincing she herself finds the competing reasons for these perspectives.[33] For example, for a person to acknowledge that there are no non-question-begging arguments that will settle the abortion debate leaves open the question of whether she believes the reasons for affirming one side or the other are superior. She might think personally that the reasons offered by both sides are equally strong or weak and thus find herself with no epistemic basis for preferring one over the other. But she might also (and probably does) believe personally that the reason(s) offered by one side – that life begins at conception or that a woman's right always overrides any fetal rights – are stronger and thus find herself with the epistemic belief that her perspective is superior.

The same holds with respect to the religious beliefs affirmed by an exclusivist. For an exclusivist to acknowledge that there exists no objective basis for adjudicating a conflict between two religious perspectives leaves open the question of how convincing she herself finds the competing lines of supportive reasoning. It is possible, of course, that she could find herself believing personally that the rational support offered by both sides is equally convincing – that is, find herself with no rational basis for preferring one perspective to the other. And I grant that if, in this case, she still chooses to affirm one as superior (more true), the best we can say is that she is not epistemically irrational to do so.

However, she might also (and probably does) find personally the rational support for one perspective more persuasive.[34] That is, she may well acknowledge that there exists no non-question-begging way to demonstrate that either perspective is superior but believe personally that the reasons for affirming the superiority of one outweigh those that can be offered for the other option. It seems to me that in this case she is fully rational (justified) in maintaining that the belief she personally finds best supported is superior – she is fully rational in holding an exclusivistic position on the conflict in question.[35]

Or to restate this important point in yet another way, to admit that there exist no non-question-begging reasons for preferring just one of two or more competing perspectives is not, as I see it, to admit that these perspectives are equally strong in the sense needed to preclude justified exclusivistic affirmation of only one.

Since Wainwright holds that a belief is 'objectively rational', as opposed to 'subjectively' rational, 'if a fully informed and properly functioning agent would hold it', he might argue that what I have defended is only subjective rationality.[36] However, I find his definition of objective rationality fatally ambiguous. Wainwright can't, I think, mean that a belief is objectively rational *only if any* fully informed and properly functioning agent would hold it. For then a person could never be fully rational in any case where no non-question-begging form of adjudication between conflicting perspectives was available. And this is a form of the very type of strong rationalism that Wainwright has rejected in other contexts.[37] What he might mean, rather, I think, is that a belief is objectively rational if any fully informed and properly functioning agent *could* hold it. Yet this is exactly the way in which I am using the term 'rationality'. So it might be that my 'subjective' definition is objective enough after all.

It could be, of course, that I have simply overlooked the sense of 'objective rationality' Wainwright has in mind. But even if this is so, I doubt any such interpretation would, or should, be accepted by all. Even more importantly, I don't see how it can be argued that the justification for continuing religious belief in the face of epistemic peer conflict is best assessed in terms of 'objective rationality'. So, while I do not claim to have shown that Wainwright is wrong (not fully justified) in holding the position he does, I find nothing in his analysis that demonstrates that my perspective on justified religious belief (in the face of peer conflict) is not equally reasonable.

Philip Quinn

In his interesting discussion of Alston, Philip Quinn offers a perspective on religious epistemic peer conflict that has not yet been considered in detail. He agrees with Alston that in the face of such conflict, an exclusivist is justified in continuing to 'sit tight' – in continuing to maintain that one's religious perspective is true. But he denies, as we shall see, that this is the only rational course of action.[38]

Quinn, like Alston, is a realist with respect to religious belief. That is, he agrees with Alston that there is a truth to the matter. However, Quinn makes a distinction between a pre-Kantian and a Kantian understanding of such belief. To have a pre-Kantian understanding of religious belief is to assume that one has (or at least can have) access to this truth as it really is. It is to believe, for instance, that one does (or at least can in principle) know what God is really like. To have a more Kantian understanding of religious belief is to assume (in my words) that although there is a literal noumenal reality, our understanding of this reality (and thus our truth claims about this reality) will of necessity be relative to the cultural/social/psychological grids through which our conceptualization of this noumenal reality is processed. It is to believe, for instance, that although there is a divine reality about which we can make truth claims, our understanding of (and thus our truth claims about) this divine reality will necessarily to some extent be conditioned by the ways in which our environment (our culture in the broadest sense) has shaped our categories of thought.[39]

Alston, Quinn contends, is essentially working off of a pre-Kantian model of religious belief when he encourages the knowledgeable and reflective exclusivist to 'do whatever seems feasible to search for common ground on which to adjudicate the crucial differences between the world religions, seeking a way to show in a non-circular way which of the contenders is correct' but to sit tight until this occurs.[40] That is, as Quinn sees it, while Alston does grant that religious exclusivists can and do over time modify their understanding of the divine reality, and even that such modification might be in the direction of greater consensus, Alston encourages exclusivists to sit tight in the face of peer conflict because he is working off of a model that presupposes that there is a knowable truth to such matters and that, in the absence of any objective basis for determining which perspective has it right, the proponent of none of the perspectives has a sufficient reason to switch to another.

Quinn does not deny that this pre-Kantian approach is justifiable and thus does not deny that someone who follows Alston's advice can be rational in doing so. However, Quinn believes that 'it should not be taken for granted that any of the contenders in its present form is correct'. Hence, he believes it is equally justifiable for an exclusivist to adopt a more Kantian approach to religious belief. Specifically, he believes it is equally justifiable for an exclusivist to assume that whatever any of us can know about the truth of the matter will never be a description of religious reality that is free of significant 'cultural' conditioning. Accordingly, it is also rational, he maintains, for exclusivists facing peer conflict to 'seek a more inclusivist or pluralistic understanding of their own faith' by modifying their beliefs to bring them 'into line with such an understanding'.[41]

In short, as Quinn sees it, Alston has left us, at least implicitly, with a false dilemma: either we find common ground on which we can objectively determine which theistic contender has the truth or we sit tight with what we have. However, Quinn argues, once we realize that it is perfectly reasonable for a person to assume that no contender has (or even could have) an accurate understanding of divine reality as it really is, another rational alternative appears. We see that it is perfectly rational for a person to begin to revise her own phenomenological perspective on the truth in a way that will allow for greater overlap with the phenomenological perspectives of others.

I think Quinn has made a significant contribution to the discussion. I agree that not all exclusivists need hold similar assumptions about our ability to access the truth. And I agree that an exclusivist can rationally seek accommodation with her competitors in exactly the Kantian manner Quinn suggests, that is, she can rationally attempt to modify her phenomenological understanding of divine reality to bring it into line with the phenomenological understandings of others. In fact, this is exactly what many exclusivists have done.

Consider, for example, the ongoing debate among Christians over how God brought the rest of reality into existence. Some claim the Bible clearly teaches that God created the 'heavens and the earth' in six twenty-four hour periods about ten thousand years ago. Others maintain that the fact that 'a day is to the Lord as a thousand years' means that while God is directly responsible for what the Bible says was created each 'day', it is most reasonable to believe that the time frame for each instance of creative activity could well have been millions, or even billions, of years. Still others continue to hold that God's direct creative activity consisted primarily of orchestrating the 'Big Bang'.

However, more recently, many Christians have taken a more Kantian approach. Based on their assumption that we may well not have access, even through Scripture, to exactly how God was involved in the creative process, they have modified what is believed to be essential to Christianity on this issue. Rather than affirming any of the specific explanations of how God created all else, they affirm a more general contention compatible with each of these specific explanations: that God is in some manner directly responsible for the existence of all else. They have, in Quinn's terms, thinned their core theologies in a way that reconciles the divergent perspectives.

But what of process theology's claim that God can unilaterally bring about nothing and thus that reality as we experience it must be viewed as God's more or less successful attempt to lure or persuade other existent entities to 'choose' to act as God would have them act? It is, of course, possible to construct an even thinner theological perspective on creation that also accommodates this view. However, is it possible for a Christian exclusivist to do so? That is, is it possible to construct a Christian theological perspective on creation that also accommodates this understanding of the creative process? The answer to this question depends on what is believed to be essential to Christianity. If a Christian exclusivist denies that unilateral creative activity is essential to Christian belief (as some do), then such accommodation is possible. However, if the Christian exclusivist believes that unilateral creative activity of some sort (perhaps creation *ex nihilo*) is essential to Christian belief (and many do), then although this exclusivist, as we have seen, may have some leeway with respect to how God's creative activity is to be interpreted, the process theology understanding of the creative process cannot be accommodated if her perspective on creation is to remain Christian.

What this highlights is the fact that Quinn's suggestion that the exclusivist move toward a thinner theology and thicker phenomenology can resolve the epistemic tension produced by peer conflict only to a certain extent. There are practical limits to Quinn's strategy. It is, as I have said, perfectly reasonable, and possibly even preferable, for exclusivists to thin their theologies (and thus thicken their phenomenologies) in an attempt to minimize that core of truths that must be accepted to remain proponents of the specific theological perspectives in question. However, to be an exclusivist – even a strongly Kantian exclusivist – is still to believe that one's religious perspective is superior. That is, it is for a person to hold not only that her perspective is in some ways incompatible with the perspectives of others but also that her perspective is in some important sense closer to the truth than are the others. Accordingly, while thinning her theology may be a rational choice that can minimize conflict, it cannot be the sole response for an exclusivist. At some point, an exclusivist must either cease to be an exclusivist or still face in some sense the choice Alston gives us: find common ground on which to determine objectively which disputant has the truth or sit tight with what she has.

The crucial difference, of course, is that for the exclusivist who has followed Basinger's Rule, this 'sitting tight' will come *after* attempting to accommodate other perspectives, not *before*. So, in the last analysis, I think that Quinn is on the right track. Even if his Kantian strategy will not (perhaps cannot) resolve religious conflict to the extent he envisions, his suggestion that the exclusivist attempt to thin her theology to minimize conflict encourages the exclusivist to consider seriously the reasons why she and her epistemic competitors hold the differing beliefs they do, which is the very type of belief assessment that I have been arguing is necessary (or at least advisable).

Moreover, as noted in Chapter 2, it has been my experience that those exclusivists who consider seriously the reasons why they and their competitors hold the differing beliefs they do very seldom end up with exactly the same set of exclusivistic beliefs they affirmed before (which I believe to be the logical outcome of sitting tight without belief assessment). Rather, these exclusivists most often find themselves with a set of modified exclusivistic beliefs to which they remain committed, beliefs that are often less restrictive, or more general, than before. They most often, in Quinn's terminology, find that their theologies have become a little 'thinner'. And this, I believe, is a practical consequence of the type of assessment I advocate that cannot be overemphasized.

Conclusion

What this chapter illustrates well, I believe, is the broad range of current philosophical perspectives on the impact of epistemic peer conflict (religious diversity) on justified religious belief. Schellenberg's position is a good example of one extreme: that unless the exclusivist can establish on objective grounds that the conflicting claims of her competitors are false, she cannot justifiably continue to claim that her perspective is superior. Wainwright offers a softened version of this position: that without a cumulative case argument for the superiority of her perspective, an exclusivist, while not necessarily irrational and while possibly pragmatically rational, cannot be fully rational epistemically in continuing to maintain that her perspective is closer to the truth than any other.

Alston's perspective exemplifies the other extreme: that since there exist no objective grounds on which to resolve disputes among basic religious perspectives, the exclusivist is not only justified in sitting tight with what she has, she ought to do so. Quinn offers a softened version of this position: that while it is justifiable for an exclusivist to sit tight in the face of diversity, it is not necessary that she do so.

My position, as noted, is closest to that of Quinn. However, while Quinn and I both believe that the exclusivist ought to do more than simply defend the right to her exclusivity, we differ somewhat on what else ought to be done. While Quinn recommends that the exclusivist consider 'thinning' her perspective in an attempt to minimize the conflict with other perspectives, my recommendation (Basinger's Rule) is more modest. My claim, again, is that while the exclusivist is indeed justified in affirming her current beliefs in the face of diversity, the reality and practical significance of such diversity gives her at the very least a good reason to assess those religious beliefs that form the core of their exclusivity.

Notes

1. As noted in Chapter 1 (note 1), since most philosophers use 'religious diversity' to label the type of epistemic tension with which this book is concerned, I normally do so also. However, given the terms in which the philosophers considered in this chapter couch their discussions, it seems to me that 'epistemic peer conflict' is the preferable descriptor for the type of epistemic tension in question.
2. For a comprehensive discussion of the various perspectives on the sufficiency of rational thought to resolve religious conflict, see Michael Peterson, William Hasker, Bruce Reichenbach and David Basinger, *Reason and Religious Belief: An Introduction to the Philosophy of Religion*, 2nd edn (New York: Oxford University Press, 1998), pp. 43–61.
3. Alvin Plantinga is, of course, also a major figure in this debate, but his perspective is discussed in Chapters 2 and 4.
4. William Alston, 'Religious Diversity and the Perceptual Knowledge of God', *Faith and Philosophy* 5 (October 1988), pp. 440–42.
5. Ibid., pp. 433–4. As we saw, though, in Chapter 1, Alston does not believe such peer conflict is as widespread as does John Hick.
6. Ibid., p. 446.
7. Ibid., pp. 442–3. As those who are familiar with Alston's work will already have noted, I have taken the liberty of modifying somewhat the exact focus of Alston's discussion. While he actually discusses epistemic peer conflict in terms of conflict between or among doxastic practices, I've portrayed him as discussing conflict between or among theistic belief systems. I've done so to keep Alston's argument more consistent with the terminology I'm using throughout this book and don't think that this in any way skews or compromises what Alston means to argue.
8. Ibid., p. 443.
9. Ibid.
10. Ibid., pp. 445–6.
11. Ibid., p. 444.
12. It might be argued that I am making too much of the peer conflict within basic theistic systems. It is true, for instance, it might be argued that while Christians differ on many interpretive issues, most Christians affirm the same set of basic tenets: that God is omnipotent, omniscient and perfectly good, etc. But while it is true that most Christians

do believe, for instance, that God is omniscient, omnipotent and wholly good, what is meant by these terms differs significantly from Christian to Christian. In fact the various meanings are sometimes contradictory. And the same is true for proponents of other basic theistic systems.

Also, it's important to note that to say that inter-system and intra-system disputes are on equal epistemic footing is not to say they are equal in every other way. For example, they aren't always of equal significance for the believer.

13. All this, it should be explicitly noted, is compatible with a conditional version of Alston's stronger claim: that disputants in debates that cannot be settled by objective means should sit tight unless or until they find themselves convinced (on subjective grounds) not to do so. This is a principle that I myself affirm in Chapter 2. It is non-problematic because this principle, unlike Alston's stronger claim, grants that there are sufficient conditions under which a person can justifiably change perspectives in the face of peer conflict, even if no objective adjudication is possible.

14. See Chapter 2 for an expanded discussion of my position.

15. J.L. Schellenberg, 'Religious Experience and Religious Diversity: A Reply to Alston', in *The Philosophical Challenge of Religious Diversity*, Philip L. Quinn and Kevin Meeker, eds (New York: Oxford University Press, 2000), p. 213.

16. Ibid., p. 213.

17. Ibid., p. 213.

18. Ibid., p. 214.

19. Ibid., p. 214.

20. Quinn and Meeker, 'Introduction: The Philosophical Challenge of Religious Diversity', in *The Philosophical Challenge of Religious Diversity*, pp. 21–2.

21. For a comprehensive discussion of strong rationalism, see Peterson et al., pp. 44–9.

22. Alston, 'Religious Diversity and the Perceptual Knowledge of God', p. 446.

23. William J. Wainwright, 'Religious Experience and Religious Pluralism', in *The Philosophical Challenge of Religious Diversity*, p. 220.

I have chosen as a general rule to discuss religious peer conflict in terms of competing religious perspectives or belief systems rather than competing doxastic practices. However, to have attempted to couch Wainwright's discussion in terms of perspectives or systems would have proved too confusing, given the number of direct quotations. As I see it, though, what Wainwright has in mind when he speaks of competing doxastic practices is what I have in mind when I speak of competing perspectives or systems. So his work fits well conceptually into the general framework of this chapter.

24. Ibid., p. 220.

25. Ibid., p. 223.

26. Ibid., p. 223.

27. William Alston, *The Epistemology of Religious Experience* (Ithaca: Cornell University Press, 1991), p. 275.

28. Wainwright, p. 222.

29. Ibid., p. 223.

30. Ibid., p. 224.

31. To say that someone is not epistemically justified in holding a belief is not, of course, necessarily to say that this person is also guilty of some sort of ethical miscue. One's ethical status with respect to beliefs is, as I see it, tied primarily to one's conscious knowledge and intent, not the epistemic status of the beliefs in question.

32. It is important to note that the question being addressed here – why a person might for pragmatic reasons want to suppress epistemic doubt – is related to, but not the same as, the earlier question of why a person might for pragmatic reasons want to engage in certain theistic practices even though she no longer believes it is epistemically rational to do so. In the earlier case, we were considering a person who has no desire to retain rational belief while, in the current context, we are considering a person who does want in some sense to preserve the belief that she is rational in considering her perspective superior.

33. I am talking here about how reasonable, in an objective epistemic sense, a person finds

the relevant arguments, and not about how affectively appealing the conclusion might be.

34. I often find in the classroom, for instance, that although students admit that there exists no objective basis for determining which perspective on God's power or knowledge is correct, they themselves firmly believe the relevant arguments to support clearly their perspectives.

35. Let me emphasize still again that I don't think that when assessing the reasons for or against the continuing affirmation of a belief (or belief system), a person must restrict herself to the consideration of propositional arguments. She can also justifiably allow as 'evidence' such things as what her experience has confirmed or what follows from other firmly held beliefs to count as relevant reasons. I believe, in fact, as stated previously, that simply the personal conviction that one perspective better organizes and explains the relevant aspects of reality is a perfectly justifiable reason to affirm it as superior, given the lack of any objective evidence to the contrary.

36. Wainwright, p. 225, note 11.

37. William J. Wainwright, *Philosophy of Religion* (Belmont, CA: Wadsworth Publishing Company, 1988), pp. 166–85.

38. Philip L. Quinn, 'Toward Thinner Theologies: Hick and Alston on Religious Diversity', in *The Philosophical Challenge of Religious Diversity*, pp. 235–43.

39. Ibid., pp. 241–2.

40. William Alston, *Perceiving God*, (Ithaca and London: Cornell University Press, 1991), p. 278.

41. Quinn, p. 242.

Chapter 4

Diversity and Pluralism

Much of the philosophical discussion of religious diversity (epistemic peer conflict)[1] continues to center on the work of John Hick. While Hick, like the philosophers discussed in the previous chapter, is interested in the question of what can justifiably be affirmed in the face of such diversity, that is not his primary concern. He is primarily concerned, rather, with the question of which justified response is most reasonable. And on this question, as we shall see, he leaves no doubt as to his opinion: religious pluralism is by far the most plausible explanation for the pervasive religious diversity we encounter. The purpose of this chapter is to clarify Hick's position and assess his defense of pluralism.

Hick's Basic Position

Hick focuses his attention on the differences between the various world religions (theistic systems). His basic pluralistic contention is not that different religions make no conflicting truth claims. In fact, he believes that 'the differences of belief between (and within) the traditions are legion' and has often discussed these conflicts in great detail.[2] His basic pluralistic claim, rather, is that such differences are best seen as 'different ways of conceiving and experiencing the one ultimate divine Reality'.[3]

However, if the various religions are really 'responses to a single ultimate transcendent Reality', how then do we account for the significant differences among these basic theistic systems?[4] The best explanation, we are told, is the assumption that this 'limitless divine reality has been thought and expressed by different human mentalities forming and formed by different intellectual frameworks and devotional techniques'.[5] Or, as Hick has stated the point elsewhere, the best explanation is the assumption that the correspondingly different ways of responding to divine reality 'owe their differences to the modes of thinking, perceiving, and feeling which have developed within the different patterns of human existence embodied in the various cultures of the earth'. Each 'constitutes a valid context of salvation/liberation; but none constitutes the one and only such context'.[6]

Initial Challenges

There continues to be a great deal of debate over what Hick really means to say about the nature of divine reality. He acknowledges that he accepts 'the distinction between, on the one hand, an ultimate and (in Kantian terms) noumenal Real *an sich* and, on the other hand, its phenomenal appearances to human consciousness as the experienced god-figures (Jahweh, Allah, Holy Trinity, Shiva, etc.) and experienced non-personal absolutes (Brahman, the Dharmakaya, the Tao, etc.)'.[7]

As George Mavrodes sees it, though, 'there is a deep ambiguity in Hick's way of thinking about the relation of the Real to the gods'.[8] One possibility is that Hick has in mind a 'disguise model'. The Real, Hick might mean, is like a prince who, wishing to travel incognito among his people, has disguised himself in different ways (for example, as a monk or stonemason). Just as what the people experience in this case are simply various appearances of the same person, the various gods experienced by humanity are actually the same divine reality, which has simply taken on different forms in the different religions. That is, on this interpretation, it is the same noumenal Real itself that is being experienced in all religions although the actual phenomenal appearance and experience of this noumenal Real is different in each religion.

The other possibility, Mavrodes continues, is that Hick has in mind a 'construct model'. Just as a number of artists painting the same landscape might create quite different representations because of the manner in which what they were viewing influenced them, it may be that none of the gods people worship is identical with the Real but are all rather human creations in reaction to some interaction with the Real. That is, on this interpretation, the noumenal Real itself cannot be experienced. Rather, what is experienced in each religion is a different phenomenal divine reality that is the product of the ways in which the noumenal Real has been constructed by human thought.[9]

Hick's response to Mavrodes is that he has neither model in mind. The disguise model correctly points out that there is only one Real, whose impact on us is experienced in different ways. However, this model incorrectly makes it appear that the Real is a god who is carrying out a divine agenda. The Real 'has no humanly conceivable intrinsic characteristics (other than purely formal linguistically generated ones) and, accordingly, is not a person carrying out a revelatory plan'.

Conversely, Hick continues, the construct model correctly notes the positive contribution of human mind to religious awareness. This model is incorrect, however, in suggesting that 'religious people directly experience the Real but respond to it by creating different concepts/images/mental pictures of it'. We do not experience the Real in and of itself. Rather, 'in religious awareness the organizing and form-giving activity of the mind operates at a pre-conscious level'.[10] We postulate the Real

> ... to satisfy (a) the basic faith that human religious experience is not purely projection but is at the same time a response to a transcendent reality or realities, and (b) the observation that Christianity, Islam, Hinduism, Buddhism etc, which are communal responses to these different gods and absolutes, seem to be more or less equally effective contexts for human transformation from self-

centeredness, with all the evils and miseries that flow from this, to a recentering in the Transcendent as experienced within one's own tradition.[11]

Critics, though, remain dissatisfied. Philip Quinn, for instance, points to the seeming inconsistency between Hick's claim that there is only one Real and his claim that the Real *an sich* cannot be said to be one or many. Quinn is also troubled by Hick's claim that we do not experience the Real in and of itself, when it appears he also holds at times that the Real in some sense transmits information to human mind and collaborates with us (albeit preconsciously) in the production of our religious experience.[12]

For our present purpose, however, we need not resolve this dispute. We are, in this chapter, assessing Hick's reasons for believing that religious pluralism offers a better explanation for diversity than does any exclusivistic alternative. And Hick himself acknowledges that neither his critique of exclusivism nor his basic argument for pluralism presupposes any particular pluralistic understanding of the Divine. His basic point, rather, is that a pluralistic hypothesis, in any of its various forms, is so much more plausible than any exclusivistic hypothesis that exclusivism ought no longer be given serious consideration.[13]

Clarification of Hick's Position

Before turning directly to a more detailed analysis of Hick's defense of pluralism, it is important that I revisit a relevant terminological ambiguity. As noted in Chapter 1, someone is a religious exclusivist, in the most general sense of the term, when she believes that her perspective on a given religious issue is alone true or is at least closer to the truth than any other perspective. And given this definition, Hick is as much a religious exclusivist as is Alvin Plantinga or William Alston in that he clearly does believe a pluralistic understanding of religious reality to be closer to the truth than any less inclusive understanding that Plantinga or Alston might want to defend. However, while many theists (for instance, Plantinga and Alston) are also religious exclusivists in the more specific sense that they believe the conceptualization of divine reality found in one religion (one basic theistic system) to be superior, Hick is not. He claims that the conceptualizations of divine reality found in many religions are equally valid (although not totally accurate) descriptions of this reality.

Moreover, it is important to keep these different senses of exclusivism in mind so we do not misunderstand what Hick is arguing. In Plantinga's critique of Hick's pluralism, Plantinga at one point makes the following claim:

> The pluralistic critic ... thinks the thing to do when there is internal epistemic parity is to withhold judgment; he knows there are others who don't think so, and for all he knows, that belief has internal parity with his; if he continues in that belief, therefore, he will be in the same condition as the exclusivist; and if he doesn't continue in this belief, he no longer has an objection to the exclusivist.[14]

Peter van Inwagen makes a similar claim:

> It is, in any case, very hard to avoid being a religious exclusivist. Professor Hick
> is himself a religious exclusivist. My religious beliefs are inconsistent with
> Islam, but so are his (and with popular Hindu polytheism and with ancestor
> worship and with ... but practically everyone in the world believes something
> that is inconsistent with his Anglo-American academic religious pluralism).
> 'Religious pluralism' is not the contradictory of religious exclusivism, but one
> more case of it.[15]

The remarks of Plantinga and van Inwagen would be a perfectly valid
response to a pluralist who claimed that she was not a general epistemic
exclusivist – who claimed that she herself was not maintaining that her
perspective was closer to the truth than any other.

However, as far as I can tell, Hick has never denied that he is a religious
exclusivist in this general sense. Nor need he, since to be a religious
nonexclusivist in the sense he intends – to deny that any one religion alone
has the correct (or most accurate) understanding of the divine – is in no way
incompatible with being a religious exclusivist in the general epistemic
sense to which Plantinga and van Inwagen are referring. That is, Hick can
grant Plantinga and van Inwagen that he is a religious exclusivist, in the
general sense they intend, without in any way weakening his contention that
those who are exclusivistic, in the more specific sense he is using this term,
are misguided.

With this distinction in mind, let us turn to an assessment of the reasons
Hick gives for finding religious pluralism the most adequate
conceptualization of reality. Before considering his explicit critique of
exclusivism, we need first to consider why Hick believes a pluralistic
hypothesis to be more plausible than the belief that there is no higher
Reality beyond us and thus that all religious claims are false – that is, why
he believes pluralism more plausible than naturalism.

Hick does not reject naturalism because he sees it to be an untenable
position. It is certainly *possible*, he tells us, that the 'entire realm of
[religious] experience is delusory or hallucinatory, simply a human
projection, and not in any way or degree a result of the presence of a greater
divine reality'.[16] In fact, since the 'universe of which we are part is
religiously ambiguous', it is not even unreasonable or implausible 'to
interpret any aspect of it, including our religious experience, in non-
religious as well as religious ways'.[17]

However, he is quick to add, 'it is perfectly reasonable and sane for us
to trust our experience' – including our religious experience – 'as
generally cognitive of reality except when we have some reason to doubt
it'.[18] Moreover, 'the mere theoretical possibility that any or all [religious
experience] may be illusory does not count as a reason to doubt it'. Nor
is religious experience overturned by the fact that the great religious
figures of the past, including Jesus, held a number of beliefs that we
today reject as arising from the now outmoded science of their day, or by
the fact that some people find 'it impossible to accept that the profound

dimension of pain and suffering is the measure of the cost of creation through creaturely freedom'.[19]

Hick acknowledges that those who have 'no positive ground for religious belief within their own experience' often do see such factors as 'insuperable barriers' to religious belief.[20] But given the ambiguous nature of the evidence, he argues, it cannot be demonstrated that all rational people must see it this way. That is, belief in a supernatural realm can't be shown to be any less plausible than disbelief. Accordingly, he concludes, 'those who actually participate in this field of religious experience are fully entitled, as sane and rational persons, to take the risk of trusting their own experience together with that of their tradition, and of proceeding to live and to believe on the basis of it, rather than taking the alternative risk of distrusting it and so – for the time being at least – turning their backs on God'.[21]

Why, though, consider pluralism the only plausible religious hypothesis? Specifically, why ought we not view religious exclusivism in exactly the same way we view naturalism? Why ought we not say that although religious pluralism is a rational choice, religious exclusivism is another religious perspective on reality that is not unreasonable or implausible to choose?

Hick does not reject this option because he believes no exclusivistic hypothesis could be true. It is certainly possible, he grants, that 'one particular "Ptolemaic" religious vision does correspond uniquely with how things are'.[22] Nor does Hick claim to have some privileged 'cosmic vantage point from which [he can] observe both the divine reality in itself and the different partial human awarenesses of that reality'.[23] However, when we consider the relevant evidence, he argues, the result is less ambiguous. Specifically, when 'we start from the phenomenological fact of various forms of religious experience, and we seek an hypothesis which will make sense of this realm of phenomena' from a religious point of view, 'the theory that most naturally suggests itself postulates a divine Reality which is itself limitless, exceeding the scope of human conceptuality and language, but which is humanly thought and experienced in various conditioned and limited ways'.[24]

What is this evidence that makes the pluralistic hypothesis so 'considerably more probable' than exclusivism? For one thing, Hick informs us, a credible religious hypothesis must account for the fact, 'evident to ordinary people (even though not always taken into account by theologians) that in the great majority of cases – say 98 to 99 percent – the religion in which a person believes and to which he adheres depends upon where he was born'.[25] Moreover, a credible hypothesis must account for the fact that within all of the major religious traditions, 'basically the same salvific process is taking place, namely the transformation of human existence from self-centeredness to Reality-centeredness'.[26] And while pluralism 'illuminates' these otherwise baffling facts, the exclusivist's response 'has come to seem increasingly implausible and unrealistic'.[27]

Finally, Hick argues, a credible religious hypothesis must account for the fact, of which 'we have become irreversibly aware in the present century, as the result of anthropological, sociological, and psychological studies and the work of philosophy of language, that there is no one universal and invariable' pattern for the interpretation of human experience, but rather a range of significantly different patterns or conceptual schemes 'which have developed within the major cultural streams'. And when considered in this light, a 'pluralistic theory becomes inevitable'.[28]

It is important to emphasize again that Hick does not intend such evidence to demonstrate that no form of exclusivism could possibly be true. However, it does seem to him so obvious that exclusivism cannot be correct, given the factors he cites. He can only conclude that those who still affirm some form of exclusivistic hypothesis really haven't considered the factors he has noted as seriously as they ought. In other words, as Hick sees it, when the exclusivist considers the type of evidence in question, the truth of a pluralistic hypothesis, or at least the inadequacy of any exclusivistic hypothesis, should become 'inevitable'.

That Hick intends here to offer a very strong challenge to the exclusivist is obvious. However, the exact nature of this challenge – what exactly he means to imply here about the epistemic status of the exclusivist – is less certain. It seems reasonable to hold that we have an epistemic duty not to affirm as true an explanation that we actually do (or should) acknowledge as much less plausible than other explanations of which we are aware. Accordingly, since Hick seems clearly to believe that all who consider the reality of diversity seriously should see that a pluralistic hypothesis is much more plausible than any exclusivistic competitor, it should not be surprising that many have interpreted Hick to be making a very strong epistemic claim: that the religious exclusivist who has considered the types of evidence he sets forth is no longer justified in retaining her exclusivistic perspective.

Plantinga's 'Reformed Epistemology' Challenge

If this is what Hick intends, there are many ways in which his claim could be challenged. What I find to be the most interesting and instructive of these responses finds its roots in the still popular 'Reformed Epistemology', first championed by philosophers such as Plantinga. I will briefly outline a standard Plantingian version of this epistemological approach and then discuss its relevance to the version of Hick's critique of exclusivism currently under consideration.

According to Plantinga, it has been widely held since the Enlightenment that if theistic beliefs are to be considered rational, they must be based on propositional evidence. It is not enough for the theist just to refute objections to any such belief. The theist 'must also have something like an argument for the belief, or some positive reason to think that the belief is true'.[29] But this is incorrect, Plantinga maintains. There are beliefs that acquire their warrant propositionally – that is, have warrant conferred on them by an evidential line of reasoning from other beliefs. And for such

beliefs, it may well be true that proponents need something like an argument for their veridicality.

However, Plantinga tells us there are also basic beliefs that do not acquire their warrant propositionally. In fact, if such beliefs can be affirmed 'without either violating an epistemic duty or displaying some kind of noetic defect', they can be considered *properly basic*.[30] And, according to Plantinga, many theistic beliefs can be properly basic: 'Under widely realized conditions it is perfectly rational, reasonable, intellectually respectable and acceptable to believe [certain theistic tenets] without believing [them] on the basis of [propositional] evidence'.[31]

What, though, are these conditions? Under what conditions can a belief have positive epistemic status if it is not conferred by other propositions whose epistemic status is not in question? The answer, Plantinga informs us, lies in a proper analysis of belief formation:

> [We have] cognitive faculties designed to enable us to achieve true beliefs with respect to a wide variety of propositions – propositions about our immediate environment, about our interior lives, about the thoughts and experiences of other persons, about our universe at large, about right and wrong, about the whole realm of *abstracta* – numbers, properties, propositions, states of affairs, possible worlds and their like, about modality – what is necessary and possible – and about [ourselves]. These faculties work in such a way that under the appropriate circumstances we form the appropriate belief. More exactly, the appropriate belief is *formed in us;* in the typical case we do not *decide* to hold or form the belief in question, but simply find ourselves with it. Upon considering an instance of *modus ponens*, I find myself believing its corresponding conditional; upon being appeared to in the familiar way, I find myself holding the belief that there is a large tree before me; upon being asked what I had for breakfast, I reflect for a moment and find myself with the belief that what I had was eggs on toast. In these and other cases I do not *decide* what to believe; I don't total up the evidence (I'm being appeared to redly; on most occasions when thus appeared to I am in the presence of something red, so most probably in this case I am) and make a decision as to what seems best supported; I simply find myself believing.[32]

And from a theistic point of view, Plantinga continues, the same is true in the religious realm. Just as it is true that when our senses or memory is functioning properly, 'appropriate belief is formed in us', so it is that God has created us with faculties that will produce true religious beliefs when working properly in a cognitive environment that is appropriate for these cognitive faculties. Accordingly, when these faculties are functioning as intended, the basic beliefs thus formed – including basic exclusivistic beliefs – can rightly be said to have 'positive epistemic status to the degree [the individual in question finds herself] inclined to accept [them]'.[33] In fact, such beliefs may have sufficient epistemic status – sufficient warrant – to justify the claim that the basic beliefs in question are known to be true.[34]

What, though, of the alleged counter-evidence to such theistic beliefs? What, for example, of all the arguments designed to demonstrate that God does not exist? Can they all be dismissed as irrelevant? Not immediately,

answers Plantinga. We must seriously consider potential defeaters of our basic beliefs. With respect to the belief that God exists, for example, we must seriously consider the claim that religious belief is mere wish fulfilment and the claim that God's existence is incompatible with (or at least improbable given) the amount of evil in the world.

However, to undercut such defeaters, he continues, we need not engage in positive apologetics: produce propositional evidence for our beliefs. We need only engage in *negative* apologetics: refute such arguments.[35] Moreover, it is Plantinga's conviction that such 'defeater defeaters' do normally exist: 'The nonpropositional warrant enjoyed by [a person's] belief in God [seems] itself sufficient to turn back the challenge offered by some alleged defeaters' – for example, the claim that theistic belief is mere wish fulfilment. And other defeaters such as the 'problem of evil', he tells us, can be undercut by identifying validity or soundness problems or even by appealing to the fact that 'experts think it unsound or that the experts are evenly divided as to its soundness'.[36]

The direct application of this Reformed Epistemology to the version of Hick's critique of exclusivism we are currently considering can be summarized as follows.

It is Hick's contention (we are presently assuming) that an objective inductive assessment of the relevant evidence makes a pluralistic thesis so much more plausible than any competing exclusivistic explanation, that continued affirmation of any such exclusivistic explanation by someone who has seriously considered all of the relevant data is unjustified.

However, it is surely possible, argues the Reformed Epistemologist, that an exclusivist's basic exclusivistic beliefs have been formed in her by faculties that are functioning properly under the appropriate conditions. For instance, it is surely possible, as Plantinga notes, that an exclusivist's beliefs have been formed by 'something like Calvin's Sensus Divinitatis, a belief-producing process that in a wide variety of circumstances functions properly to produce [exclusivistic] belief'.[37]

Moreover, it is surely possible, continues the Reformed Epistemologist, that the reason why so many others do not affirm these same exclusivistic beliefs is because their faculties are not working as they ought to work (perhaps because of some physiological defect) or because these individuals are not in the appropriate environment (perhaps because they were raised in a cultural context not conducive to truth production). For example, if we confine ourselves to Christian exclusivism, perhaps the reason why so many see it differently is because the Christian exclusivist has been graced by 'the Internal Witness of the Holy Spirit', who 'preserves the Christian church from serious error, at least with respect to the fundamentals of Christian belief' or that he 'has been converted by divine grace, so that he now sees what before was obscure to him – a blessing not so far bestowed upon the dissenters'.[38]

Furthermore, adds the Reformed Epistemologist, to defeat the claim that her exclusivistic beliefs are unjustified, an exclusivist need not demonstrate in relation to some objective standard of plausibility that her exclusivistic

perspective is the most plausible explanation for the diversity we experience. To defeat this challenge, an exclusivist need only argue successfully that Hick has not shown that all must agree that a pluralistic explanation is so much more plausible that continued affirmation of her exclusivistic beliefs is unjustified. That is, it is not enough for Hick simply to say that he firmly believes a pluralistic explanation to be vastly superior or that he firmly believes that all thoughtful, honest people should agree. The burden of proof is on him to demonstrate that a pluralistic explanation is vastly superior in some objective sense that will allow no one justifiably to disagree.

However, this line of reasoning continues, Hick offers us no set of objective criteria on which his comparative assessment is based. Nor is it likely he could. As Plantinga and others have convincingly argued, the plausibility of any specific explanation for a set of data is relative to the plausibility of one's basic background beliefs – to one's basic metaphysical commitments concerning the nature of reality.[39] And it is widely acknowledged (even by Hick himself) that there exist no objective, non-question-begging criteria for adjudicating epistemological differences among basic metaphysical perspectives.

Accordingly, concludes the Reformed Epistemologist, Hick's alleged defeater of exclusivistic belief – that a pluralistic explanation for the diversity we experience is comparatively so plausible that the retention of exclusive belief is unjustified – can itself be considered defeated. So not only is it the case that an exclusivist can justifiably continue to affirm her exclusivistic beliefs, she is, in fact, even justified in maintaining that she knows the contentions in question to be true.

It seems to me that in a very important sense the Reformed Epistemologist is correct. It is certainly possible that we possess religious belief-forming faculties that produce true beliefs when functioning properly under the appropriate conditions. And I agree that there exists no set of non-question-begging criteria in relation to which it could be demonstrated objectively that a pluralistic explanation is significantly more plausible than an exclusivistic explanation based on the existence of such faculties. So I agree that the Reformed Epistemologist does offer the exclusivist an adequate defence for her exclusivity. Furthermore, since it is clearly the case that there are some philosophers (even if Hick is not actually among them) who continue to maintain that the reality of religious diversity renders exclusivistic belief unjustified, the availability of such a defence is significant.

However, it is important to note that this response to Hick – a response based on the nature of our belief-forming faculties – may be of value to fewer exclusivists than Reformed Epistemologists such as Plantinga believe. As Plantinga acknowledges, a defence of justified, warranted belief based on properly functioning belief-forming faculties will be successful only if the purpose of the 'epistemic faculties producing the belief in question is to produce true beliefs'.[40] And although Reformed Epistemologists clearly believe this to be the case, the assumption that our religious belief-forming faculties, even if created by God, were actually intended to produce true belief can reasonably be challenged.

In an interesting analogous discussion on the function of conscience, Bertrand Russell questions the claim that the dictates of conscience should be considered, even in principle, to be an accurate indicator of appropriate ethical behaviour. He acknowledges that we have a conscience – an 'ethical faculty' that produces in us the feeling that what we are about to do (or have done) is right or wrong. However, he denies that the purpose of this faculty is to indicate what actually is right or wrong – to produce true ethical belief. As he sees it, the purpose of a properly functioning conscience, rather, is simply to assess our behaviour in terms of whatever set of ethical beliefs we happen to hold at the time, whether such beliefs are actually true or not.[41]

In like fashion, it might be held – even by a staunch exclusivist – that the cognitive faculties that produce in us our basic religious beliefs were never intended (even by God) to produce in us true belief, but were intended, rather, only to produce belief consistent with the basic beliefs of the environment (the general cultural, family and/or church setting) in which these faculties function. In other words, it might be held that the cognitive faculties that produce in us our basic religious beliefs could be functioning properly even if their aim is not the production of truth. A Christian exclusivist might argue, for instance, that the reason why the Bible so adamantly instructs parents to 'train up a child in the way he shall go' is just because the truth-producing capacity of our belief-producing faculties – even when functioning properly – is so dependent on the context in which they function.

Now, of course, an exclusivist need not accept this interpretation of proper functionality. But I see no reason why an exclusivist could not plausibly do so. And for those who do view the function of religious belief-producing faculties in this manner, the Reformed response to the pluralistic challenge in question, by Plantinga's own admission, won't do.

However, an exclusivist need make no assumption about the nature of our cognitive faculties to utilize the general defensive strategy employed by the Reformed Epistemologist. As we have seen, to argue successfully that a pluralistic explanation for the reality of religious diversity is so plausible that exclusivistic belief is unjustifiable, it must be demonstrated objectively (on the basis of criteria acceptable to all parties) that this is so. However, Plantinga and others are right, I think, to argue that there exists no current interpretation of 'justified belief' or 'warranted belief' on the basis of which the superiority of a pluralistic explanation can be argued. And this is true apart from any additional assumption about the intended purpose of our belief-forming faculties. Hence, even if an exclusivist doesn't assume that our religious belief-forming faculties are intended to be truth-producing, she can still maintain that exclusivistic belief is justified in the face of diversity.

Does Hick, though, really mean to argue that the implausibility of exclusivist belief renders such belief unjustifiable? Is this really his intended critique of exclusivism? I don't think so.

As Plantinga and other Reformed Epistemologists openly acknowledge, the line of reasoning they employ to defend exclusivistic belief can, in principle, be employed justifiably by exclusivists of any religious persuasion, even though the basic theistic systems in question are clearly incompatible. The strongly exclusivistic Christian is in no better or worse epistemic position than is the strongly exclusivistic Muslim or Jew or Hindu or Buddhist. Each can, in principle, justifiably maintain that her exclusivistic beliefs are true (possibly even known to be true) and thus that the incompatible beliefs held by others are false.

Accordingly, as I see it, the reality of religious diversity actually raises at least two significant questions for the exclusivist:

Q1: Can an exclusivist, in the face of religious diversity, justifiably retain her exclusivistic perspective?

Q2: Given that all exclusivists are, in principle, on equal epistemic footing – given that all can claim justifiably that their exclusivistic perspectives are true – why should the proponent of any given exclusivistic perspective continue to believe that her defensible perspective is superior?[42]

While most of the philosophers we have considered clearly focus on Q1, Hick, I am convinced, is primarily interested in Q2. His language, I admit, can make it appear at times that his goal is to challenge an affirmative response to Q1 – to claim that no one can justifiably remain an exclusivist. However, he himself has, pointedly, denied that this is so. For instance, in a response to an article in which I explicitly argue that Plantinga is concerned primarily with Q1 and Hick primarily with Q2, Hick acknowledges in relation to Q1 that 'the epistemologist of religion *can* adopt exclusivist theological theories'. Moreover, in this same context, Hick responds to my attempt to distinguish his primary concern from Plantinga's in terms of these two questions by stating that he believes this comparative assessment not only 'to be correct', but also a 'very helpful constructive contribution'.[43]

However, if Hick's focus isn't really Q1 – the question of whether an exclusivist can retain justified belief – but rather Q2 – the question why an exclusivist would in the face of diversity want to retain her exclusivistic belief – then what exactly does he mean when he claims that a serious consideration of all the relevant data related to diversity makes a pluralistic explanation 'inevitable'? What he is giving us, I think, is primarily his personal conviction that anyone who seriously considers the 'facts of the matter' will inevitably agree with him that a pluralistic explanation for the religious diversity we experience is clearly superior to any exclusivistic alternative. Or, stated in more general terms, Hick's challenge to exclusivism is best read, I believe, as an invitation to consider seriously the various reasons why some choose one justified explanation for diversity over another, along with his firmly held belief that anyone who does so will see it his way.[44]

My Critique

Assuming this reading of Hick to be correct, let us, accordingly, turn our attention to the evidential debate itself. Has Hick given us persuasive reasons to consider a pluralistic hypothesis superior to any exclusivistic competitor?

One of Hick's evidential claims, remember, focuses on the concept of transformational parity. After noting that a credible hypothesis must account for the fact that within all of the major religious traditions 'basically the same salvific process is taking place, namely the transformation of human existence from self-centeredness to Reality-centeredness', Hick argues that while pluralism persuasively 'illuminates' this otherwise baffling parity, the strict exclusivist's view 'has come to seem increasingly implausible and unrealistic'.

There has been, and will continue to be, debate over whether the same basic personal transformation actually does occur within various religions; over whether there is real transformational parity. Kelly Clarke, for instance, grants that an exclusivist can never justifiably deny such parity on the basis of behavioral observation. However, he argues,

> Suppose ... that I am a practitioner of a particular religion. I have been taught my beliefs by my parents and other adults that I respect from childhood onwards. I have participated in liturgy that reinforces my views on the transformative powers of reality and feel cleansed, made whole and at peace with reality. I see significant spiritual transformation in the lives of those who are members of my community. I read literature and holy writ that attest to and confirm my view of reality. I develop my beliefs about both the goal and the process of transformation and these beliefs are arguably justified for me. Now suppose that I am in a position where I must judge whether or not other religious traditions are equally transformationally effective. Surely I will not be forced, by dint of experience, to judge that people whose practices and goals are widely divergent from mine are just as successful at putting them in touch with Ultimate Reality and attaining transformation. I will almost certainly question their beliefs and practices, find them strange, perhaps bizarre, and most likely believe them to be mistaken. My antecedent commitments prevent me from judging that my belief competitors are just as transformationally successful as my beliefs.[45]

In short, as Clarke sees it, while an exclusivist can never justifiably deny that there is actual transformational parity among diverse religious perspectives on the basis of experience alone, she can justifiably deny such parity if the denial follows from (or is required by) other beliefs within her perspective that she justifiably affirms.

I think that Clarke is correct. Proponents of many basic theistic systems do claim that while transformational parity may appear to be the case, this is actually not so: do claim that the transformation within their systems actually is qualitatively different than that produced by allegiance to other systems. It is sometimes argued, for instance, that the transformation within other systems will not last, or at least that this transformation, while maybe real and even lasting for a given individual, is not what it could have been for that individual within the 'true perspective' in question. And, although I believe personally that transformational parity is a reality, I agree that since the exclusivist can justifiably affirm the superiority of her basic system, she can justifiably deny that such parity actually exists. In other words, if the question is whether the proponent of a given exclusivistic perspective can justifiably deny actual transformational parity, the answer would appear to be yes.

However, by Clarke's own admission, the proponent of any exclusivistic system can, in principle, justifiably deny transformational parity: can justifiably claim that transformation within her system is actually superior. And even Clarke acknowledges that there exists no objective, non-question-begging way of demonstrating that one perspective is actually correct. Accordingly, if the question is whether the proponents of any exclusivistic perspective can demonstrate on grounds common to all that transformational parity does not exist, the answer then appears to be no.

Moreover, and more importantly for our purposes, not all exclusivists deny transformational parity (even though they justifiably could). Within Christianity, for example, increasingly large numbers of even very conservative adherents (I know from experience) don't claim that their perspectives have any greater transformational power. They don't claim, for instance, that Christianity produces 'changed lives' to a greater extent than other religions or that 'changed' Christians are 'better' people. They emphasize, rather, that what sets Christianity apart from the rest is the fact that Christianity is the truth.

Accordingly, let us assume for the sake of argument that Hick is right about transformational parity. Let us assume that while there clearly is a considerable range of actual transformation within each religious perspective, significant and similar transformation does occur within all the major religious traditions. Is Hick, then, also right to assume that only pluralism can plausibly illuminate these facts?

I agree that a pluralistic hypothesis – the assumption that all religious perspectives are connecting their adherents to the same transforming divine reality – does offer us a reasonable explanation for such transformational parity. That is, it seems to me that a pluralistic hypothesis is a plausible explanation for the similar transformational power of various religious perspectives.

However, I disagree with Hick's stronger claim: that the exclusivist who acknowledges transformational parity, but denies that this is the result of the work of the same divine reality, has no plausible alternative explanation to offer. Hick, of course, recognizes that such exclusivists do have various non-pluralistic hypotheses available. He recognizes that they can (and do) argue, for instance, that transformational parity is the result in part of the documented power of people committed to the efficacy of some 'change agent' to 'change themselves' – that they can (and do) attribute transformation in adherents of other religions to the power of positive thinking. And he recognizes that such exclusivists can (and sometimes do) acknowledge the efficacy of a supernatural agent but claim that the agent in question is an evil force (for instance, Satan) who is trying to keep the adherents of other religious perspectives from the truth by making it appear that there is no need to search elsewhere. However, Hick, as we have seen, considers such exclusivistic explanations totally inadequate. Not only do they strike him as implausible, but he also believes that any sincere, honest person considering the facts of the matter should agree that such responses are 'unrealistic'.

It seems to me, though, that Hick has failed in this context to take into account the epistemic principle on which, as we have seen, exclusivists such as Plantinga and Clarke base their response to his evidential challenges: that the plausibility of any specific explanation for a set of data is relative to the relevant basic background beliefs. To help illustrate this point, let us consider the following version of a scenario first introduced in the previous chapter.

One night Bill, who has been dating Sue for some time, passionately informs her that she is truly the only love of his life. But later that night, while looking out of her window, Sue sees someone who appears to be Bill walking down the street with his arm around another woman, and thus finds herself wondering whether Bill was telling her the truth. What Sue would like, of course, is an unambiguous *explanation* – an explanation that is subject to objective verification. She would like to discover, for example, that the young man was not really Bill or that, if it was Bill, the woman was his sister who had arrived unexpectedly.

However, what if it was Bill and he cannot offer an unambiguous explanation? What if the woman was one of Bill's former girlfriends and he tells Sue that he was simply walking with her one last time to inform her that their relationship was finished and had his arm around her to 'soften the blow'? That is, what if Bill offers an explanation that is not subject to objective verification? Or what if Bill offers no explanation at all? What if Bill, when confronted, tells Sue that he is not at liberty to offer an explanation or does not believe he can offer one that she will fully understand and then asks that she simply believe that things are not as they seem – simply believe that there is a sufficient reason for his behaviour?

Would it then remain reasonable (realistic, plausible) for Sue to continue to believe she is in fact Bill's only love? The answer, as I see it, depends on the nature of the other relevant beliefs concerning Bill that Sue holds. If she, in fact, has little reason to believe Bill tells the truth in such contexts – if, for example, this is not the first time something like this has happened – then it may well be implausible (unrealistic) for her to believe Bill in this case. But what if Bill's moral character is beyond reproach? What if, for instance, everyone agrees that Bill always tells the truth, and this has, in fact, always been Sue's experience? The situation is then different. Most of us, I believe, would then appropriately acknowledge that it would be reasonable (realistic) for her to continue to believe that Bill loved only her, even if no clear explanation (or no explanation at all) were available.

In short, to generalize, we must distinguish between plausibility claims that are contextual and those that aren't. To claim that a statement or hypothesis is contextually plausible is to claim that it is reasonable or realistic, given certain relevant background beliefs, while to claim that a statement or hypothesis is non-contextually plausible is to claim that it is reasonable or realistic, apart from any relevant background beliefs.

Hick, it seems to me, wants us to consider exclusivistic explanations for transformational parity in a non-contextual manner. That is, it appears that he wants us to position ourselves as objective observers of this debate and ask ourselves the following question: if we consider only the fact that many of the world's religions appear by almost any standard to have equal transformational power, what is the most plausible explanation? Is it most plausible to assume that all such transformation is the result of connection with the same divine transformational source or to assume that some such parity is self-induced or the result of connection with a malevolent force?

Considered in this way, Hick's contention that only a pluralistic hypothesis seems credible (reasonable or realistic) appears to me correct. If we were to consider as neutral observers only the fact (currently being assumed) that many of the world's religions have equal transformational power, then it does seem to me few of us would opt for some sort of exclusivistic response. However, exclusivists need not consider this transformational question in isolation from other relevant, basic beliefs. Christian exclusivists, for example, need not consider this transformational question in isolation from their belief that the Bible is the authoritative word of God and that the Bible teaches us that while those in other religions can experience maximal transformation, only in the Christian faith is this solely or primarily brought about by connection with the divine. In any such case, Hick's pluralistic hypothesis must be considered in relation to both the exclusivistic hypothesis itself and the set of background beliefs out of which it arises.

Moreover, if we do so, the situation changes considerably. For then, to claim that his pluralistic explanation for seeming transformational parity is the only credible, reasonable, realistic choice, Hick must demonstrate not only that a pluralistic hypothesis is sufficient to outweigh the plausibility of any exclusivistic competitor simpliciter. He must also demonstrate that the plausibility of a pluralistic hypothesis is sufficient to outweigh the plausibility of the whole set of basic beliefs in which this exclusivistic hypothesis is embedded. And it isn't at all clear to me that this claim will have much appeal, even to the neutral observer. In other words, even if we grant Hick that a pluralistic hypothesis seems clearly preferable to any exclusivistic competitor when considered in isolation, I'm not certain that even neutral observers will believe a pluralistic hypothesis to be so strong that it renders implausible the sets of basic background beliefs to which these exclusivistic explanations for seeming transformational parity are related.

It is important, though, that this critique of Hick be kept in perspective. Since I believe that there exists no objective basis on which to deny the reality of transformational parity, and Basinger's Rule mandates (or at least strongly recommends) belief assessment when peer conflict cannot be resolved objectively, I am in total agreement with the weaker Hickean claim that seeming transformational parity does require the exclusivist to question her exclusivistic perspective. And such assessment, as I have argued, may well lead to some belief modification. It could even cause an exclusivist to reject her current explanation for such parity. What I am challenging at present is only Hick's stronger claim: that a pluralistic explanation is so inherently plausible that anyone seriously considering the options really ought to agree that the affirmation of any exclusivistic alternative is unreasonable or unrealistic or implausible.

Moreover, whether or not I am correct on this point, Hick's use of seeming transformational parity to support pluralism runs into another type of difficulty. Hick, understandably, has us focus on the question of whether various religious perspectives seem equally successful in transforming the lives of adherents – in changing adherents from 'self-centeredness to Reality-centeredness'. However, there is, it seems to me, another important question to ask in this context, namely whether there are explicitly non-religious perspectives that are equally successful in transforming people in a similar fashion. That is, does our observation of human behaviour give us reason to believe that the same sort of transformation in attitude and behaviour that takes place within various religions also takes place outside of any such religion?

The answer, I believe, is clearly yes. I remember, for instance, attending a peace rally in 1968 at which Dr Benjamin Spock, then already a very successful, wealthy individual, gave his 'testimony'. Yes, he acknowledged, he did have fame and fortune although his life had for some time been empty, devoid of significant purpose. However, he continued, his commitment to the peace movement had changed all that. It had produced in him a concern for others that had given his life new meaning and value. He had, we were told, been transformed.

Stories such as this abound. People making a 'secular' (non-religious) commitment to some goal, value, or metaphysical perspective – be it concern for the environment or disease or world hunger or emotional health – often appear to have their lives transformed in ways quite similar to the ways in which the lives of religious believers are transformed. They, too, appear to change from self-centeredness to a focus on reality outside of self.

If this is so, however, Hick's pluralistic hypothesis runs into a powerful non-religious competitor: the contention that the religious transformational parity we correctly observe is simply a subset of the general transformational parity we observe among individuals who commit themselves to any perspective on life that centers reality outside of self, and thus that it is much more plausible to assume that all religious transformational parity is the result of some form of internal conceptual realignment rather than the result of some sort of connection with an external divine reality.

It might be argued in response, of course, that the type of transformation that takes place within a religion is not really the same as that which takes place outside of religion, but I see no objective basis on which such a claim could be substantiated. Or, it might be argued that this seemingly 'secular' transformation is really the result of some sort of connection with the divine. However, again, I see no objective basis for such a contention.

Accordingly, it seems to me that Hick faces a dilemma. If he admits that equal transformation can and does actually take place outside of connectedness with the divine, then he greatly weakens his claim that connectedness with the divine is the most plausible explanation for religious transformation. However, if he wants to argue that all (or most) true transformation is the result of connectedness with the divine, even though there may be little objective evidence that this is the case, then it is hard to see how he can justifiably view as implausible the exclusivist's claim that all transformation outside of her religion is the result of something other than connectedness with the true God primarily because there is little objective evidence that this is the case. So, again, while I think transformational parity (inside and outside of religion) must rightly be considered seriously by the exclusivist, I don't see such parity as a decisive argument against the plausibility of exclusivistic belief.

Another of Hick's evidential claims focuses on the fact that 'religious allegiance depends in the great majority of cases on the accident of birth: someone born into a devout Muslim family in Pakistan is very likely to be a Muslim, someone born into a devout Hindu family in India to be a Hindu, someone born into a devout Christian family in Spain or Mexico to be a Catholic Christian, and so on'. That this is so, he is quick to add, does not 'show that claims to a monopoly of religious truth are unjustified'.[46] However, it does force us to ask the following question: 'Can we be so entirely confident that to have been born in our particular part of the world carries with it the privilege of knowing the full religious truth, whereas to have been born elsewhere involves the likelihood of having only partial and inferior truth?'[47]

Or as he states this question in another context: 'Can one suppose that the Heavenly Father, who loves all human beings with an equal and unlimited love, has ordained that only those who have the good fortune to be born in certain parts in the world shall have the opportunity of salvation?'.[48] Since, as Hick sees it, the obvious answer is that we cannot reasonably make this assumption, he concludes that the basis for the affirmation of any exclusivistic hypothesis is greatly weakened.

Plantinga, however, views this line of reasoning as 'another philosophical tar baby'. The sociological fact that people tend to have the religious beliefs of the culture in which they are raised can, he acknowledges, 'produce a sense of intellectual vertigo'.[49] He is even willing to admit that 'no matter what philosophical and religious beliefs we hold and withhold (so it seems), there are places and times such that if we had been born there and then, then we would not have displayed the pattern of holding and withholding of religious and philosophical beliefs we *do* display'.[50]

However, it doesn't follow from this, he argues (or believes it can be argued), that we ought not accept the religious views that we have been brought up with or that the belief-producing processes that have produced these views are not reliable:

> For suppose we concede that if I had been born in Madagascar rather than Michigan, my beliefs would have been quite different ... the same goes for the pluralist. Pluralism isn't and hasn't been widely popular in the world at large; if the pluralist had been born in Madagascar, or medieval France, he probably wouldn't have been a pluralist. Does it follow that he shouldn't be a pluralist or that his pluralistic beliefs are produced in him by an unreliable belief-producing process? I doubt it.[51]

In fact, it isn't obvious to Plantinga that we can, on the basis of the undeniable correlation between religious belief and place-time of birth, 'infer *anything at all* about what has warrant or how we should conduct our intellectual lives'.[52]

In response, Hick first grants that Plantinga is correct in one respect: it doesn't follow from the fact that one would probably hold different beliefs if one had been raised somewhere else that one is not justified in holding one's present beliefs. However, Hick sees Plantinga's 'Madagascar' comparison to be irrelevant to his claim that the exclusivist should find the high correlation between place-time of birth and religious belief troubling: 'One is not usually a religious pluralist as a result of having been raised from childhood to be one, as (in most cases) one is raised from childhood to be a Christian or a Muslim or a Hindu, etc.'. So surely, Hick argues, 'the cases are so different that the analogy fails'.[53]

Plantinga, though, remains unconvinced. He is, first of all, dissatisfied with Hick's desire for us to think only about 'the beliefs with which [we are] brought up, not just any beliefs [we have]'.[54] But even if we restrict ourselves to the consideration of the former, Plantinga argues, Hick's contention that the high correlation between place-time of birth and beliefs should give the exclusivist pause can be rejected:

> No doubt Hick, like me, was brought up to believe that racial intolerance is wrong. Now it is fairly likely that most relevant place-times are such that if he and I had been brought up there and then, we would have quite different views on this topic. Does that mean that we should eye our tolerance with special suspicion? Maybe we should; but if, after careful, prayerful thought and consideration, it still seems to us that racial intolerance is wrong, unjust, and morally repugnant, there is nothing arbitrary in our continuing to reject racism. But then why should it be different for Christian belief?[55]

It seems to me that both Hick and Plantinga are right and wrong. Plantinga's basic goal here, as elsewhere, is clearly to defend exclusivistic belief from the charge that it is unjustified or irrational. In this he succeeds by default. Even Hick acknowledges that it does not follow from the high correlation between place-time of birth and religious belief that the religious exclusivist is not justified in retaining her exclusivistic perspective in the sense of justification Plantinga intends.

Hick's main goal, on the other hand, is to cause the exclusivist to question whether she should continue to affirm with confidence her exclusivistic perspective, given the correlation in question. And here, I think, he basically succeeds although I don't think his argument is as clear as it could be.

Hick is surely correct when he states that most religious individuals affirm the dominant religious perspective of the culture in which they were raised. However, such individuals can be divided into two relevant categories: those who have compared the origins and content of their culturally bestowed beliefs with the origins and content of competing religious perspectives and those who haven't. For example, we can divide those Muslims who were raised in Islamic cultures into two categories: those who have compared their religious perspective with the competing religious perspectives of Christians, Hindus, etc., and those who haven't.

This distinction is important because the key problem posed by religious diversity is not, as I see it, simply that there is diversity of religious thought; simply that individuals (or groups of individuals) *do* in fact affirm differing religious perspectives. The real problem, rather, is that *seemingly sincere, equally knowledgeable* individuals hold differing perspectives. That is, what does (I think properly) generate concern is the fact that those who have thought seriously about significant religious issues, given the same relevant data and arguments, *still differ* on what is true.

Accordingly, if we read Hick as simply pointing out that most people have lived and died affirming the dominant religious perspective of the culture in which they were raised, then what he has to say is of little relevance to our discussion of religious diversity. However, it seems clear that Hick's argument is based on a stronger claim: that even with respect to those sincere individuals who have been exposed to other perspectives, there still exists a very high correlation between place-time of birth and the specific religious perspective held. What Hick wants to emphasize, I believe, is that most sincere, knowledgeable religious individuals who have been raised in Islamic cultures, for example, still affirm some form of Islamic belief, and that the same is true of most knowledgeable Hindus or Christians or Jews.

And the fact that this is so, it seems to me, is a valid reason to question the superiority of any specific perspective. Just as the incompatible testimony of seemingly sincere, equally trustworthy witnesses who were both at the scene of an accident does rightly give authorities or jurors a reason to question the reliability of any of the witnesses, the high correlation between place-time of birth and religious perspective among those who are seemingly sincere and operating out of the same knowledge base should, I believe, give an exclusivist reason to pause. For instance, this correlation does, I believe, give the Reformed Epistemologist a reason to question whether we as humans do possess reliable religious belief-producing faculties and, if so, whether such faculties are intended to produce truth.

I'm not certain, though, that Plantinga necessarily disagrees with this point. In his direct response to Hick, Plantinga clearly wants to downplay the significance of the place-time of birth/current religious belief correlation. But the actual thrust of the challenge in question, as Hick himself clearly acknowledges, is not to deny that 'a knowledgeable, thoughtful, and ethically sensitive Christian exclusivist, such as Plantinga himself, is morally as well as intellectually entitled to his exclusivistic faith'.[56] That is, what Hick is arguing is not that the correlation in question renders exclusivistic belief unjustified in the sense that to remain a religious exclusivist, given this correlation, is to violate some epistemic duty. What Hick wants to argue, rather, as I am interpreting him, is that reflection upon the high correlation in question should have a very significant negative impact on the exclusivist's confidence in the superiority of her exclusivistic perspective.

Understood in this manner, I see this challenge as simply one important example of the intellectual tension produced by what Plantinga calls 'the enormous variety of human religious response'. And Plantinga himself believes, as already noted, that awareness of such diversity often directly reduces, at least initially, an exclusivist's 'level of confidence or degree of belief', sometimes to the point where it deprives the exclusivist of knowledge of what he believes.[57]

It is, of course, true that Plantinga does not see this negative impact as necessarily permanent. In fact, he believes, remember, that a thoughtful reconsideration of one's exclusivistic beliefs in light of such a challenge may result in a strengthened exclusivistic stance. However, the fact that Plantinga acknowledges that thoughtful reconsideration may be required clearly shows, I think, that he does not really want to maintain that the challenge I am claiming Hick thinks the high place-time of birth/religious belief correlation poses for exclusivists is a 'philosophical tar baby'. Rather, if we interpret Hick's challenge as I maintain it should be interpreted, then I think that Plantinga himself would at least agree that it is of significance – that Hick has indeed identified an important *prima facie* challenge to exclusivistic belief.

Or, to restate in slightly different terms what I have been attempting to argue about the disagreement between Plantinga and Hick over the high place-time of birth/religious belief correlation, it seems to me that this disagreement can at least in part be attributed to the fact that they are not talking about the same epistemic issue. Plantinga reads Hick's challenge in terms of Question 1 – the question of whether an exclusivist can, in the face of diversity, retain her exclusivist perspective. In response, accordingly, he argues that awareness of the correlation in question does not render exclusivistic belief unjustified. But this, as we have seen, is not something with which Hick disagrees. Hick, on the other hand, is interested in Question 2 – the question of whether an exclusivist should continue to affirm her justifiable exclusivistic perspective, given the reality of pervasive religious diversity. The key to his response is his claim that the high correlation in question should negatively affect the degree of confidence the thoughtful exclusivist will have in her exclusivistic perspective. But this, I have maintained, is not something with which Plantinga really disagrees.

Where Plantinga and Hick really do differ is with respect to the force of this challenge – the degree to which the high place-time of birth/religious belief correlation will (should) negatively affect an exclusivist's confidence. Hick believes that a pluralistic explanation for this high correlation should be seen by any thoughtful person as clearly the only credible option. Plantinga believes, as I am here interpreting him, that while acknowledgment of this correlation can minimize an exclusivist's confidence in the credibility of her exclusivistic perspective, it certainly need not do so to the extent Hick claims it should.

My own position is clearly closer to Plantinga's at this point. I am willing to grant that if we were to consider as neutral observers the high correlation between place-time of birth and religious allegiance in isolation, a pluralistic explanation might well seem to most of us to be most plausible. However, plausibility, as we have seen, is a subjective concept relative primarily to one's relevant background beliefs. Accordingly, exclusivists need not consider the high place-time of birth/religious belief allegiance correlation in question in isolation from other relevant beliefs. For example, the Christian exclusivist need not consider this correlation in isolation from her basic belief that the Bible is an authoritative source of truth and that the Bible teaches that only the Christian perspective contains a totally accurate view of reality. Moreover, it seems to me that the exclusivist is (or at least can be) justified in viewing the plausibility of such relevant background beliefs as outweighing the seeming counter-evidence posed by the correlation in question. Hence, I disagree with Hick's contention that a pluralistic explanation for the correlation in question is really the only plausible option for sincere, objective individuals.

However, let me re-emphasize, I do believe that the high place-time/religious belief correlation is, indeed, a valid reason for any exclusivist to reassess her exclusivism. And while the result of this assessment will not in most cases be conversion to pluralism, such assessment may well in at least some cases result in a 'thinner theology'. It may well result in an exclusivism in which the set of incompatible beliefs among the various exclusivistic perspectives has been minimized. So such assessment can be significant.

This brings us to Hick's final piece of evidence. Hick holds, remember, that a credible religious hypothesis must account for the fact, of which 'we have become irreversibly aware in the present century, as the result of anthropological, sociological and psychological studies and the work of philosophy of language, that there is no one universal and invariable' pattern for the interpretation of human experience, but rather a range of significantly different patterns or conceptual schemes 'which have developed within the major cultural streams'. And when considered in this light, Hick concludes, a 'pluralistic theory becomes inevitable'.

In part, Hick is again surely correct. There clearly is no universal and invariable pattern for the interpretation of human experience. As acknowledged earlier, the place-time in which one is born clearly does dictate in part the way in which one organizes and explains reality. Does this, however, make the rejection of any exclusivistic religious perspective inevitable? I certainly agree that the tremendous effect of culture on how one interprets reality is a very important factor for the exclusivist to consider. However, is it true that once the exclusivist admits that culture shapes reality, she is no longer in a position to claim plausibly that her religious perspective is in fact superior?

I don't think so. While it is clearly true that our understanding of the power of cultural conditioning has increased, it is also clearly true, as Hick himself acknowledges, that proponents of the major religions recognize this fact and offer self-consistent responses. That is, Hick is quite aware of the fact that proponents of most religious traditions acknowledge the shaping influence of culture on religious belief. And he is aware of the fact that they offer what they see as sufficient responses to the reality of such cultural conditioning – for example, that other cultural perspectives are the result of the significant shaping power of malevolent forces or that those in other cultures have not yet had a chance to hear 'the truth'.[58]

As Hick sees it, though, such exclusivistic responses to the shaping effects of culture on religious belief are so obviously *ad hoc* that no thoughtful person should find them convincing. The much more reasonable response, he believes, is simply to assume that no single religious perspective is superior.

However, as we have seen in relation to the other evidence Hick cites, when comparing the plausibility of specific beliefs, we must consider not only these specific beliefs themselves but also the basic background beliefs in which they are embedded. And that this is so greatly weakens Hick's argument – his claim that a pluralistic explanation for the shaping power of culture on religion is inevitable. For even if we grant that a pluralistic response to the obvious shaping power of culture is preferable to any exclusivistic response when considered in isolation, it isn't at all clear to me that even neutral observers will see Hick's hypothesis as so strong that it renders implausible the whole set of basic background beliefs out of which the exclusivist's response to the profound shaping influence of culture on religious belief arises. Hence, I simply don't see how it can be said, as Hick does, that affirmation of the pluralistic response to the obvious impact of culture on the shaping of religious reality – namely, the pluralistic contention that no specific cultural/religious interpretation of reality can be considered superior – becomes inevitable.

Before concluding this discussion of Hick's evidential case for pluralism, I want to make one final comment about the overall strength of this line of reasoning. Hick argues that since the exclusivist can offer no plausible response to the transformational parity among religions, high correlation between place-time of birth and religious belief, and the shaping power of culture on religious belief, pluralism is the inevitable choice.

However, this seems to me to be a false dilemma. As was noted earlier, one can be a non-exclusivist – deny that only one specific religious system contains more truth about the divine than any other – without being a pluralist – without making the additional positive claim that there does exist a divine reality that manifests itself partially, but equally, in many religious traditions.

So the question arises: Even if Hick has given us good reasons to reject exclusivism, has he given us good reasons to accept pluralism? And I think the answer to this question is no. Consider, for example, Hick's claim that the high correlation between place-time of birth and religious affiliation is best explained by pluralism, by assuming that the divine can be experienced equally in various religious traditions. Even if we agree that this high correlation is a good argument against exclusivism, the contention that pluralism best explains this correlation only holds if there exists no equally plausible non-exclusivistic, non-pluralistic explanation.

However, I think such an explanation is available. Even Hick agrees that there exists no objective way to resolve most conflicts among religious perspectives. Accordingly, it might well be argued by a non-exclusivist that the reason for the high correlation in question has little to do with the nature of the divine but is rather a function of the fact that whenever sincere, knowledgeable religious individuals find no objective reason to change allegiances – find that attempts at objective adjudication do not produce a definitive winner – significant numbers are likely to retain some version of the religious perspective with which they are most familiar. Hick, of course, might not find this non-exclusivistic, non-pluralistic explanation as plausible as his own. But since he gives us no reason why this explanation can't be considered equally reasonable, it does stand, I think, as a barrier to his claim that the high correlation in question is best explained by pluralism.

Or consider Hick's claim that our current understanding of the tremendous shaping power of culture on our interpretation (including our religious interpretation) of reality makes the acceptance of a pluralistic theory 'inevitable'. I see nothing in Hick's discussion that would prohibit a non-pluralistic non-exclusivist from arguing in an equally justifiable manner that what the shaping power of culture points to, if anything, is not that there exists some divine reality that can be experienced through all religions – that pluralism is true – but rather only that it is unlikely that any specific cultural tradition can claim to have the truth – that exclusivism is false.

And, as we have already seen, while Hick claims that the transformational parity among religions points clearly to a single divine transforming power, it appears just as plausible, given anything Hick has said, to make the non-exclusivistic non-pluralistic assumption that what transformational parity demonstrates most clearly is the tremendous transformational power of serious commitment to anything outside of self.

In short, it seems to me that Hick has tried to prove too much. I agree (let me emphasize again), that the experiential factors he has identified do give the exclusivist good reason to engage in the type of belief assessment Hick desires. However, even if such assessment did require the rejection of exclusivism (which I have argued is not the case), Hick has not given us sufficient reason to embrace pluralism. He has at best given us only a sufficient reason to affirm some form of non-exclusivism.

Conclusion

To summarize, then, what has been argued in this chapter is that the reality of religious diversity raises at least two important, but distinct questions: can the exclusivist justifiably continue to affirm her exclusivity? And, if so, does she really want to do so?

With respect to the first question, there is, I have maintained, really no disagreement. Exclusivists such as Plantinga argue that they can justifiably continue to claim that their specific religious perspectives are superior to all others, but this is not something with which pluralists such as Hick disagree.

However, with respect to the question of whether any exclusivistic explanation for religious diversity can actually be considered more plausible than (or at least as plausible as) a pluralistic explanation, we do have a true difference of opinion. Hick, as we have seen, believes the evidence supporting a pluralistic explanation to be so convincing that he simply can't understand how anyone seriously and openly considering the issue could see it differently. Exclusivists, though, correctly point out that the plausibility of any given explanation for diversity must be considered in relation to the background beliefs in which it is embedded. And when considered in this light, I have maintained, exclusivists need not grant that a pluralistic explanation is more plausible than their own.

However, that this is so, it must be re-emphasized, is not incompatible with my claim that the reality of diversity obligates the exclusivist to assess her beliefs. Nor is it incompatible with my contention that such assessment may often lead an exclusivist to a 'thinner' – more pluralistic – theological perspective. What I have argued in this chapter is only that the exclusivist need not be epistemically apologetic if, after such assessment, she continues to believe her specific religious perspective to be superior.

Notes

1. As noted in Chapter 1 (note 1), since most philosophers use 'religious diversity' to label the type of epistemic tension with which this book is concerned, I normally do so also.
2. John Hick, 'On Conflicting Religious Truth-Claims', *Religious Studies* 19 (1983), p. 487.
3. John Hick, 'The Philosophy of World Religions', *Scottish Journal of Theology* 37 (1984), p. 229.
4. Ibid., p. 229.
5. John Hick, 'The Theology of Religious Pluralism', *Theology* (1983), p. 335.
6. Hick, 'The Philosophy of World Religions', pp. 229, 231.
7. John Hick, 'The Epistemological Challenge of Religious Pluralism', *Faith and Philosophy* 14 (July 1997), p. 283.
8. George Mavrodes, 'Polytheism', in *The Rationality of Belief and the Plurality of Faith: Essays in Honor of William P. Alston*, Thomas D. Senor, ed. (Ithaca and London: Cornell University Press, 1995), p. 272.
9. Ibid., p. 272.
10. Hick, 'The Epistemological Challenge of Religious Pluralism', p. 284.
11. Ibid., p. 284–5.
12. Philip L. Quinn, 'Toward Thinner Theologies: Hick and Alston on Religious Diversity',

in *The Philosophical Challenge of Religious Diversity*, Philip L. Quinn and Kevin Meeker, eds (New York: Oxford University Press, 2000), p. 233.

13. Hick, 'The Epistemological Challenge of Religious Pluralism', p. 285.
14. Alvin Plantinga, 'Pluralism: A Defense of Religious Exclusivism', in *The Philosophical Challenge of Religious Diversity*, p. 182.
15. Peter van Inwagen, 'A Reply to Professor Hick', *Faith and Philosophy* 14 (July 1997), p. 300.
16. John Hick, *Why Believe in God?* (London: SCM Press, Ltd, 1983), pp. 43–4.
17. Ibid., p. 67.
18. Ibid., p. 34.
19. Ibid., pp. 64, 100.
20. Ibid., p. 100.
21. Ibid., p. 67.
22. Hick, 'The Theology of Religious Pluralism', p. 338.
23. Ibid., p. 336.
24. Hick, 'The Philosophy of World Religions', p. 231.
25. John Hick, *God Has Many Names* (London: Macmillan Press, Ltd, 1980), p. 44.
26. Hick, 'The Philosophy of World Religions', p. 231.
27. Hick, *God Has Many Names*, p. 49.
28. Hick, 'The Philosophy of World Religions', p. 232.
29. Alvin Plantinga, 'The Foundations of Theism: A Reply', *Faith and Philosophy* 3 (July 1986), p. 307.
30. Ibid., p. 300.
31. Alvin Plantinga, 'On Taking Belief in God as Basic', Wheaton College Philosophy Conference (October 1986), Lecture I handout, p. 1.
32. Alvin Plantinga, 'Justification and Theism', *Faith and Philosophy* 4 (October 1987), pp. 405–406.
33. Ibid., p. 410.
34. Plantinga, 'Pluralism: A Defense of Religious Exclusivism', p. 190.
35. Plantinga, 'The Foundations of Theism', p. 313, n. 11.
36. Ibid., p. 312.
37. Plantinga, 'Pluralism: A Defense of Religious Exclusivism', p. 189.
38. Alvin Plantinga, 'Ad Hick', *Faith and Philosophy* 14 (July 1997), p. 296.
39. Alvin Plantinga, 'The Probabilistic Problem of Evil', *Philosophical Studies* 35 (January 1979), pp. 1–53.
40. Plantinga, 'Pluralism: A Defense of Religious Exclusivism', p. 189.
41. Bertrand Russell, 'A Sense of Sin', in Robert E. Dewey and Robert H. Hurlbutt, eds, *An Introduction to Ethics* (Macmillan, 1977), pp. 128–34.
42. Even Plantinga acknowledges that this is an important question.
43. John Hick, 'A Concluding Comment', *Faith and Philosophy* 5 (1988), p. 451.
44. Portions of the preceding comparative discussion of Hick and Plantinga first appeared in 'Plantinga, Pluralism and Justified Religious Belief', *Faith and Philosophy* 8 (January 1991), p. 67–80.
45. Kelly James Clarke, 'Perils of Pluralism', *Faith and Philosophy* 14 (July 1997), p. 316.
46. Hick, 'The Epistemological Challenge of Religious Pluralism', p. 281.
47. Ibid., p. 281.
48. Ibid., p. 282.
49. Plantinga, 'Pluralism: A Defense of Religious Exclusivism', p. 187.
50. Ibid., p. 188.
51. Ibid., pp. 187–8.
52. Ibid., p. 188. This line of reasoning appears in a context in which Plantinga is explaining how someone who holds a reliabilist account of knowledge might responsd to Hick. But while Plantinga's own 'proper functionalism' differs in some respects from reliabilism, what he argues the reliabilist can say seems to me clearly to be what he believes to be true.
53. Hick, 'The Epistemological Challenge of Religious Pluralism', p. 281.

54. Plantinga, 'Ad Hick', p. 298.
55. Ibid., p. 298.
56. Hick, 'The Epistemological Challenge of Religious Pluralism', pp. 280–81.
57. Plantinga, 'Pluralism: A Defense of Religious Exclusivism', p. 189.
58. In fact, proponents of those theistic perspectives that have a strong tradition of proselytization – for example, Christianity and Islam – often find in such responses strong motivation for their evangelistic efforts.

Chapter 5

Diversity and Eternal Destiny
of Humankind

As is evident from the preceding chapters, contemporary analytic philosophers of religion normally discuss the reality of religious diversity (epistemic peer conflict)[1] in quite general terms. Specifically, the key questions considered are whether an exclusivist can, in the face of diversity, justifiably retain her exclusive perspective and why, even if she can, she should want to continue to do so. However, there is at least one specific issue that a number of contemporary analytic philosophers of religion who are interested in religious diversity have addressed directly: the traditional exclusivistic Christian claim that while 'true Christians' will spend eternity in a state of conscious bliss with God (heaven), many, if not most, non-Christians (except possibly for children) will spend eternity in a conscious state of damnation (hell).

Initial Clarifications

It is first important to note that not all Christians make this exclusivistic claim. For instance, some Christians simply deny that there is any literal afterlife or acknowledge that there is a conscious state of eternal bliss for the 'saved' but maintain that the 'damned' are simply annihilated – they cease to exist.[2] Richard Swinburne is an example of a well-known Christian philosopher of religion in this latter category. God, he maintains, would not punish someone beyond what this person deserves, and everlasting physical punishment would exceed such deserts, making God vindictive rather than just. It is also true, though, Swinburne argues, that there is no 'point of keeping a totally corrupt being alive. He has lost the center of his being. There would be no point in giving him the "vision" of God, for he could not enjoy it'. And for such a person, Swinburne suggests, annihilation is appropriate since God has no obligation to keep anyone in existence.[3]

Still other Christians acknowledge the actual existence of both a heaven and a hell but reject the contention that many will spend eternity in hell. They affirm instead some form of universalism – the belief that while some or even many begin the afterlife in hell, all, or at least the vast majority, will eventually exist in heaven permanently.[4]

However, many Christians do still affirm the traditional exclusivistic claim in question – do still claim that many, if not most, non-Christians will spend eternity in hell. And these Christians, not surprisingly, encounter significant criticism by those of other faith perspectives – a significant challenge at the inter-system level. For instance, non-Christians often pose some version of the Hickean challenge noted in the last chapter: Given that many, if not most, people historically have never had the opportunity to hear the Christian message, and given that how we interpret reality (including religious reality) is strongly shaped by the culture in which we are raised, how, it is argued, could anyone maintain that all those who aren't Christians are consigned to eternal damnation? In fact, these critics conclude, this question is so significant that without a reasonable response the plausibility of traditional Christian exclusivism is at the very least greatly weakened.[5]

Moreover, even within Christian circles – even at the intra-system level – significant debate exists. For instance, while all Christians affirming the exclusivistic claim in question agree that 'true Christians' will spend eternity in God's presence, there is significant debate over which categories of non-Christians, if any, will also be allowed in God's presence and the sufficient conditions under which this will be so.[6]

My goals in this chapter are two-fold. I will first outline and assess the various attempts by traditional Christian exclusivists to clarify and/or defend the claim that many will spend eternity separated from God. Second, I will share how I think this specific debate highlights some important aspects of the general diversity discussion.

Traditional Explanations

Can the traditional Christian exclusivist (hereafter referred to simply as the traditional exclusivist) offer a plausible explanation for the claim in question? Specifically, can she explain how a fair, just, loving God could condemn to hell those who have not accepted him?

It must first be noted that some traditional exclusivists don't even attempt to offer an explanation that non-Christians or Christians who are not traditional exclusivists will find reasonable or plausible.

Some traditional exclusivists, for instance, deny that our basic human understanding of justice and fairness has its origin in God's nature and, thus, deny that such moral concepts can justifiably be applied to discussions of God's activity. They maintain, instead, that since God is under no obligation to act in accordance with those principles that we as humans have considered central to moral behaviour, any attempt to offer an explanation for God's seemingly unfair soteriological standards that non-Christians or non-traditional Christians will find plausible is misguided and, should, therefore, be avoided.[7]

Second, even some Christians who believe it is legitimate, in principle, to utilize our human understanding of fairness and justice in assessing divine activity argue that we ought not to search for a plausible response to the soteriological challenge in question since they believe that in this specific case we are incapable, in principle, of identifying an adequate response. Specifically, these paradox theists, as they are sometimes called, believe that the love of God and the reality of hell are two of the truths 'taught unmistakably in the infallible Word of God' and that since these two truths 'cannot possibly be reconciled before the bar of human reason', there is little else to be said.[8]

Finally, those traditional exclusivists who are theological determinists do have within their system an unambiguous response to the question of how a loving God could allow many to spend eternity in hell. Since they believe that God can bring about any logically possible state of affairs, including any logically possible set of free choices, they are committed to the claim that God consigns many to hell because a world in which he does so (this world) is on balance a better world than any other world God could have actualized, including any world in which no one spends eternity separated from God. Even they realize, though, that this is an explanation that very few non-Christians or Christians who are not determinists will find plausible from a human perspective.[9]

However, many traditional exclusivists – in fact, I think the clear majority at present – are theological indeterminists. That is, they deny that God can both grant a person freedom and yet control the decision-making process. And some in this category have wanted to offer what they see as plausible responses to the question of how God could allow many of his creatures to be separated eternally from him. While such responses, as we will see, differ significantly, most begin with some form of the following argument.

All humans are born in a sinful state, a state of alienation from God that prohibits them from being in God's presence since God cannot cohabitate with sin. However, God, in his love, sent Christ to pay the price for their sins – to establish an avenue whereby sinners can enter into a proper relationship with God. Thus, anyone who acknowledges that he or she is a sinner and accepts Christ's propitiatory act is reconciled with God and, accordingly, will spend eternity in God's presence.

However, God has chosen to give humans meaningful freedom with respect to salvation, and God cannot both grant a person freedom and determine how it will be utilized. Thus though God deeply desires all to be in heaven, even he cannot force individuals to acknowledge freely their sin and accept the 'gift of salvation' made possible through Christ's redemptive act. Moreover, it happens to be the case, unfortunately, that many will choose freely to reject God. Accordingly, the fact that many who have lived on earth will ultimately be numbered among the damned does not count against either God's power or goodness.[10] Rather, 'hell is [simply] the place provided by a long-suffering God for those who refuse to go His way. Having tried all to win them, God will ultimately have to say to some, "All right, have it your way"'.[11]

In a conditional sense, this initial response continues to appear adequate to many. *If* we assume that individuals must spend eternity in either heaven or hell and that God cannot force people to make the decisions necessary to enter heaven, then the fact that some (or even many) freely choose not to be reconciled with God, and thereby end up in hell, is not seen as counting strongly against God's goodness.

However, it seems an indisputable fact, as frequently noted, that many individuals have died without the opportunity either to accept or to reject God's plan of salvation. Specifically, many 'children' have died before developing the capacity to conceptualize the options necessary to make a meaningful decision, while many 'adults' who had the capacity to decide for or against Christ have died without having had access to the gospel.[12] What is the eternal destiny of this sizeable portion of humanity? Do they automatically spend eternity in hell because they have never freely accepted God's 'way of salvation'? Do they automatically spend eternity in heaven because they have never freely rejected God? Or are other criteria relevant in such cases?

Traditional exclusivists have long been aware of this issue and have responded in various ways. The question concerning the fate of those who die in early childhood (or die having possessed only the mental capacities of young children) is least controversial at present. Historically, the eternal fate of such children was often seen as conditional. Some Christians held that God 'elected' some for heaven and allowed the rest to spend eternity in hell. Others held that the deceased children of all believers were allowed to enter heaven. Still others claimed that the salvation of children who died was tied to the sacrament of baptism.[13] Today, though, almost all traditional exclusivists have a 'softer' stance. They maintain that all those who die in early childhood (or die having possessed only the mental capacities of young children) are automatically allowed to spend eternity with God.[14]

One might expect, accordingly, that such reasoning would also apply to those individuals who are capable of accepting or rejecting God but have never heard the gospel. However, this is not usually the case. Many traditional exclusivists still maintain that the teachings of Scripture clearly prohibit them from believing that those in this category also automatically enter heaven.[15]

But how can this be fair? It is one thing to say that those who have freely chosen not to reconcile themselves to God will spend eternity outside of God's presence. However, how can it be fair to say that many of those who had the capacity to accept or reject God's plan of salvation but never the opportunity to do so are also condemned, especially when all who die as young children are allowed to enter heaven?

The traditional exclusivists in question are also well aware of this problem, and while various responses are possible, the one utilized by most today is based on what is seen as a significant dissimilarity between those who are not capable of accepting or rejecting God and those individuals who are capable of accepting or rejecting God but have never heard the gospel.

It is true, it is granted, that those in neither category can respond to the gospel. In addition, though, to God's self-revelation in Christ – God's Special Revelation – God has also revealed himself in nature – God's natural revelation. That is, God has so constructed us and the world we experience that his existence as creator and sustainer is evident to everyone capable of accepting or rejecting him. Moreover, everyone in this category has been granted the freedom to establish a personal relationship with God at some level – to commit as much as she knows of herself to as much as she knows of God. Thus, while young children are free of responsibility (and thus bound for heaven if they die) because they are not capable of accepting or rejecting God, those capable of responding to God can still be viewed as responsible for their eternal destiny. They are judged on the basis of how they respond to that natural revelation that is available to them.[16]

In other words, although the traditional exclusivists in question still believe that humans can be reconciled with God only because of Christ's atonement for sin on the cross, they hold that the eternal destiny of those who have never heard the gospel is ultimately based on how these individuals respond to that truth to which they do have access. And, accordingly, in the minds of such traditional exclusivists, the character of God remains unassailable.

However, most of these traditional exclusivists also believe that while God's natural revelation is sufficient to make all responsible for their eternal destiny, God's Special Revelation – the gospel – is much more effective. That is, they also believe that those who hear the gospel are much more likely to respond positively.[17] But if this is true, then an additional question immediately arises: how can an all-loving God justly allow those who have never had the opportunity to respond positively to the gospel spend eternity in hell?

Traditional exclusivist Jerry Walls has recently responded by denying that God's grace is necessarily confined to the earthly realm. Some people, he grants, are in a position to accept or reject Christ freely in this life. And for such people, their eternal fate is sealed when they die. But with respect to those who have never heard the gospel or have never clearly understood it, he argues, God's perfect goodness entails that 'there may be further opportunity at death' to hear the gospel and thus receive salvation.[18]

Another, more recent option is offered by Jonathan Kvanvig. God, he argues, is essentially good and, as such, is committed to preserving both our existence and our rational freedom of choice (our ability to decide freely among options open to us). However, since we are dependent on God to sustain our existence, we ultimately have only two options: to accept freely dependence on God (which is to choose continued existence) or to reject dependence on God (which is to choose nonexistence). Because of his goodness, God sustains all persons (allows them to exist) for as long as is necessary for them to come to the point where they can make a rational, settled choice between God and nonexistence. And those who choose God will remain in existence with God in the heavenly community. However, even though God is committed to preserving our existence, God is even more strongly committed to our rational freedom. Thus those who ultimately make a rational choice to be independent of God (and thus choose not to exist) will be allowed by God to annihilate themselves in this fashion. But it is also possible that some may never come to the place of accepting or rejecting God. And it is consistent with God's goodness, Kvanvig believes, for him to allow these individuals to 'eternally exist in hell', a state of existence which 'is as bad as anything can be (compatible with God's perfect goodness)'.[19]

However, the vast majority of traditional exclusivists in question – the vast majority of those who deny that the 'unevangelized' can automatically enter heaven – continue to believe that one's decisions *in this life* are decisive with respect to one's eternal destiny.[20] Thus, for these traditional exclusivists, the question remains: If God is all-loving, how can he justly allow those who have never heard the gospel to spend eternity in eternal torment?

The Significance of God's Knowledge

It is at this point that some traditional exclusivists claim that God's knowledge becomes relevant. Specifically, some claim that certain models of omniscience (certain conceptualizations of divine knowledge) are an asset when attempting to produce a plausible response to the challenge at hand, while others claim that such models are a liability in this context.

In order to establish a common ground for this discussion, I will begin by outlining the three relevant models of omniscience and identifying the distinctions between them.[21]

Some traditional exclusivists believe that God possesses what is currently labelled 'present knowledge'. They believe that God knows all that has occurred in the past, is occurring now, and that which will follow deterministically from what has already occurred. However, they deny that God necessarily knows all that will occur in the future. Specifically, they argue that since God cannot control how humans utilize their freedom, God does not know exactly what will come about as the result of those freely made decisions that have not yet been made.[22] They maintain, for example, that since God cannot control human freedom, then to the extent that he has decided to allow the next US presidential election to be decided by human decision-making, he does not know with certainty who will in fact be elected.

Other traditional exclusivists believe that God possesses what is currently labelled 'simple foreknowledge'. They believe that God knows not only what has occurred and is occurring but also all that will actually occur in the future, including what all individuals will freely choose to do. They believe that God knows, for example, who will be elected as the next U.S. President even though he will not control the decision-making involved.

But there is yet another way in which some traditional exclusivists conceive of God's knowledge. They believe that God possesses what is labelled 'middle knowledge'. That is, they believe that God knows not only what has happened, is happening, and will actually happen in the future, but also what every individual would freely do in every possible situation in which that individual could find himself or herself. Or stated differently yet, they believe that God knows the modal profile of every possible person. If Ted Kennedy had been elected in 1980, God knows, for example, if, faced with this option, he would have chosen freely to run for US President in 1984. And God knows now not only who will be elected in the forthcoming US presidential election and what decisions she or he will make, but also who the other candidates will be and exactly what they would have done if they had been elected.

These models can be contrasted in many ways, but for the purpose of our present discussion, the relevant distinction centers on how much God knew about this world before his decision to actualize it. If God possesses only present knowledge, then creation was, in a very real sense, a risk. God did not know exactly what would result from his creative decision. Specifically, God did not know with certainty who would freely choose to accept or reject either the gospel or his natural revelation.

If God possesses simple foreknowledge, then things are slightly different. Since God knows now all that will happen in this world, nothing surprises God now; he is not now taking any risks. However, before God decided (logically speaking) which of the numerous creative options open to him – which actualizable world – to initiate, there was no actual world. Thus, since a God with simple foreknowledge knows only what will actually occur in the future, until he had decided which creative option to initiate, he had no way of knowing exactly what would occur given the actualization of any of these options. Specifically, God had no way of knowing to what extent the free choices made would be in keeping with his will. Even more specifically, he again had no way of knowing with certainty who would freely choose to accept or reject the gospel or his natural revelation.

Things are quite different, however, if God possesses middle knowledge. He then knew before creation exactly what would occur in every world he could bring into existence, including how each individual would respond freely to God's natural revelation or the gospel in any conceivable situation in which she could find herself. This doesn't mean, it must be emphasized, that a God with middle knowledge could, therefore, necessarily have brought it about that any possible person could have been among the elect simply by actualizing a world in which the appropriate conditions held. For if God cannot control the free actions of individuals, then it could be that some individuals would never freely respond positively to God, given any set of conditions. But if God possesses middle knowledge, then he did know before the actualization of this world not only who would and would not freely choose to respond positively to God's natural revelation or the gospel under the conditions found in this world, but also which of those who would not respond positively to God under the conditions found in this world would respond positively under some other set of possible conditions.

In short, the key distinction between these models has to do with the extent to which creation was a soteriological gamble. If God possesses present knowledge or simple foreknowledge, then God did not know before the creation of this world (logically speaking) who would respond positively (and thus ultimately be in heaven) and who would not respond positively (and thus ultimately be in hell), while if God possesses middle knowledge, then this information was available to him.

With this in mind, let us return to the question facing most traditional exclusivists: How can a just God allow anyone to go to hell who has not had the actual opportunity to hear the gospel?

Hunt's Challenge

David Hunt has argued that although this is a serious challenge for any traditional exclusivist, it is a much more serious challenge for the traditional exclusivist who believes God possesses middle knowledge.[23] It is true, Hunt acknowledges, that the proponent of middle knowledge has a slight advantage with respect to a related issue: creative risk. While the traditional exclusivist who denies that God possesses middle knowledge can legitimately be asked to explain why a God who did not know before creation who would spend eternity in hell would have risked creating our world, the traditional exclusivist who affirms middle knowledge needs no such explanation since a God with middle knowledge took no such risk. He knew before creation exactly who would or would not be among those damned eternally.

However, Hunt is quick to add, this type of prior knowledge creates enormous difficulties when considered in relation to the question of why some who have never heard the gospel are eternally damned. Specifically, he argues, such knowledge makes it very difficult (if not impossible) for the proponent of middle knowledge to explain why God created any sort of pre-mortem, earthly existence at all. If God does not have middle knowledge, and thus did not know who would accept or reject the gospel before creation, then it can at least be argued that a pre-mortem existence was necessary to determine who would be among the elect. However, if God knew before creation not only who would not respond positively to the gospel under any possible set of circumstances, but also who would accept the gospel under some possible set of circumstances, then, as Hunt sees it, there is no reason why an all-loving God would not simply have actualized 'a world consisting of nothing but eternal felicity for the elect, omitting pre-mortem life with all the ... evil it entails'?[24]

Or, stated differently, it is Hunt's contention that although the traditional exclusivist who denies middle knowledge may find it difficult to respond to the question of how God can allow those who have never heard the gospel to spend eternity in hell, the traditional exclusivist who affirms middle knowledge is left with no justifiable response at all. For if God possesses middle knowledge and is omnibenevolent, then there is no reason why he would not simply have identified those individuals who he knew would have responded positively to the gospel if given a chance and actualize them directly into a heavenly state, thus circumventing the need for eternal damnation altogether.

Hunt recognizes that this line of reasoning doesn't hold if God had some justifiable reason for arranging a pre-mortem existence. For example, Hunt tells us, a proponent of middle knowledge might argue that

(1) 'The elect need to have actual experiences of trials and temptations' before they enter heaven.[25]

But (1), we are told, does not help the proponent of middle knowledge. First of all, Hunt points out, most Christians today believe that those who die at a very young age automatically go to heaven. They reason that 'though [those who die very young] never accept Christ, they never reject Him either' so 'God in His graciousness therefore receives them into heaven.'[26] But this is obviously inconsistent with (1). For if young children don't need 'actual experiences of trials and temptations' to enter heaven, then why do any of the rest of us?

Second, Hunt argues, even if we assume that (1) is correct in the sense that the elect do need to have 'actual experiences of trials and temptations', there is no good reason to believe these experiences must involve the damned. The elect themselves, he believes, could generate enough 'trials and temptations' to do the job. And, even if this were not so, we are told, the 'role of the damned (which is solely to elicit experiences in the elect)' could be 'played by perfect simulacra' (soulless replicas).[27] To create such simulacra, he grants, would involve deception on God's part. The elect would not know they were interacting with soulless beings. However, the stakes are so high, he believes, that in this case – namely, when considering the eternal torment of the lost – such deception would be morally justified.

Or, to state his basic point more directly, it is Hunt's opinion that an all-loving God who could have created such replicas – and thereby avoided the necessity of hell – would obviously have done so. Consequently, he concludes that the traditional exclusivist who affirms middle knowledge is still left with no reasonable response to the question of why some of those who will never hear the gospel will spend eternity in hell since it is still the case that, given middle knowledge, this question should not even arise.

Hunt has certainly raised an interesting challenge, but it seems to me that a traditional exclusivist who affirms middle knowledge has an adequate response available. In fact, this response has in a very real sense been furnished by Hunt himself. After arguing (correctly) that the proponent of middle knowledge cannot claim that a pre-mortem existence is necessary for the purpose of identifying who will be among the damned or saved, Hunt acknowledges, remember, that 'God may have some other reason for arranging a pre-mortem existence for us'.[28] But he discusses only one such reason – the possibility that the trials and temptations encountered in a pre-mortem existence are necessary to prepare the elect for a blessed eternity – and then goes on to argue that this reason will not suffice.

However, a traditional exclusivist who affirms middle knowledge need not grant that this is the only reason (or even a reason) why she believes God has actualized a pre-mortem existence. Most exclusivists do, of course, believe that the trials and temptations in this life can strengthen our character. And some may believe that such trials do help prepare some for heaven. However, the contention that the reason why the damned exist is to prepare believers for an afterlife is certainly not a common belief among traditional exclusivists. In fact, I doubt that many would even consider it orthodox. Accordingly, in response to Hunt's specific challenge, it is perfectly justifiable for the traditional exclusivist who affirms middle knowledge to maintain that a pre-mortem existence is necessary (and has in fact been actualized) for some other reason than the one Hunt dismisses.

But couldn't Hunt (or someone else) simply adapt his critique to any such reason? I think not. Let us first reconsider Hunt's 'fate of the child' objection. Hunt assumes that traditional exclusivists want to affirm both that a pre-mortem existence is necessary for the elect and that children who die very young go to heaven automatically. He then argues that these two contentions are inconsistent because if children don't need a pre-mortem existence, then there is no reason to think that such an existence is needed by anyone bound for heaven.

The traditional exclusivist, as we have seen, can easily deflect this specific challenge by simply denying that the reason we have a pre-mortem existence is to prepare the elect for heaven. However, a more generalized tension of this sort might be thought to remain, given any reason that a traditional exclusivist who affirms middle knowledge might offer for the existence of a pre-mortem world: if God, in his graciousness, receives into heaven those young children who, although they have never accepted Christ have never rejected him either, then why cannot God automatically receive into heaven all those who have never rejected him because they have never heard (or clearly heard) the gospel?

This is an important question. However, this is not a question generated, or even exacerbated, by middle knowledge, for the issue here is not what God knows but rather the seemingly different criteria being utilized by God to judge those in the two categories under consideration. That is, the question of why God seemingly does not apply the same soteriological standards to those who die in childhood as he does to those who have never heard the gospel is not affected by the type of knowledge God is thought to possess. All traditional exclusivists, regardless of what model of omniscience they affirm, face exactly the same challenge here. Hence, since Hunt's goal is to demonstrate that it is much more difficult for the proponent of middle knowledge to explain how a just God could allow the unevangelized to spend eternity in hell, raising the question of why God cannot treat the unevangelized as he does children will not help Hunt in this context.

This still leaves, though, Hunt's second objection: the contention that if the damned are required to furnish the elect with the trials and temptations required to prepare them for heaven, then the same good could have been achieved by creating soulless human replicas to serve this function *incognito*. This specific criticism, as we have seen, also collapses because the traditional exclusivist who affirms middle knowledge can simply deny that Hunt has accurately identified the reason for a pre-mortem existence. But again it might be argued that a variation remains: Given any reason for a pre-mortem state of existence that a traditional exclusivist might stipulate, wouldn't an all-powerful, all-loving God who knew before creation exactly who would spend eternity in hell still have replaced such individuals with exact soulless replicas?

This, too, is an interesting question, but one for which the traditional exclusivist who affirms middle knowledge has a response available. She can deny that an all-loving God would have created non-humans who look and act like humans by arguing that the intrinsic value of significant freedom is such that a world like ours – a world in which all who function as humans do actually possess significant freedom although some spend eternity in hell – is a better world on balance than one in which only the elect possess significant freedom and no one suffers eternal torment.

Is such a response adequate? Hunt (and others) may well find it 'inexplicable'.[29] However, this response is not self-contradictory or incompatible with other beliefs traditional exclusivists affirm. Accordingly, if this response is to be rejected, it will have to be because this line of reasoning in question is so implausible that no one seriously considering this issue could justifiably find such a response adequate. As we have seen in the previous chapter, however, there exist no objective criteria for 'plausible belief' in relation to which claims of this type can be made. Hence, while Hunt and others are perfectly free to consider the response in question inexplicable, I see no reason why the traditional exclusivist cannot justifiably disagree.

Moreover, I can think of no other basis on which it might be argued that traditional exclusivists who affirm middle knowledge cannot justifiably acknowledge that an all-loving God did in fact find it necessary to create a pre-mortem existence for both the saved and the damned. Accordingly, we must conclude, I believe, that while Hunt has raised some interesting, important questions, he has not demonstrated in an objective manner that the proponent of middle knowledge cannot offer an adequate response to the problem of 'eternal damnation' – an adequate response to the question of why an all-loving God would allow some who have never heard the gospel to spend eternity in hell.

Craig's 'Middle Knowledge' Defence

Traditional exclusivist William Craig, however, wants to go even further. He claims not only that middle knowledge does not exacerbate this problem, as Hunt believes, but that, given middle knowledge, a very fruitful response becomes available.[30] If God could have created a world in which many individuals freely choose to accept him and none reject him, Craig begins, he certainly would have done so. (Craig is here assuming that God would prefer a world containing many saved and some lost to a world containing only a few saved and none lost.) But it is possible that in every actualizable world containing many individuals who freely choose to accept God, there also exist some individuals who freely choose to reject him.

Moreover, it is possible, Craig continues, that all of those individuals who have not responded positively to God in the world God has chosen to create

– and are thus bound for hell – are individuals who God knows, via middle knowledge, 'would not freely receive Christ under any circumstances' for example, 'no matter how much the Spirit of God worked on their hearts, no matter how favorable their upbringing, no matter how many times and ways they heard the gospel'.[31]

Or, to state this last point more formally, it is possible, according to Craig, that all who are lost in this world suffer from transworld damnation. That is, 'it is possible that they would have been lost in any world in which God created [them]'.[32] And assuming that this is so, Craig concludes, an answer to the question of how a just God could allow some individuals who have never heard the gospel to spend eternity in hell becomes obvious: it is possible that there are no such persons. That is, it is possible that God did ensure that all who would have accepted the gospel in this world had the opportunity to do so in the sense that if this world had been known by God prior to creation to contain anyone who would not respond positively to God under the circumstances found in this world, but would have responded positively to the gospel under any other possible circumstances, God would not have actualized this world.[33]

Furthermore, not only is all this possibly true, Craig argues, it is 'quite plausible ... as a soteriological theodicy'. That is, Craig believes not only that this middle knowledge response to the soteriological challenge at hand allows traditional exclusivists to defend themselves against charges of logical inconsistency but also that it is a perspective that traditional exclusivists can quite reasonably believe mirrors reality – can believe is actually true.[34]

Is Craig correct? Has he outlined a promising response for the traditional exclusivist who affirms middle knowledge? Before addressing this question directly, I want to investigate one tangential aspect of Craig's position: his assumption that 'God would [very probably] prefer to create a world in which many people are saved and a few lost than to create a world in which a handful of people are saved and nobody lost'.[35] This assumption is one that many proponents of middle knowledge might well challenge, and it is not essential to Craig's basic argument. If one were to assume instead that when God chose to actualize this world, the only actualizable creative options contained both some saved and some damned (which even Craig doesn't deny might have been the case), whatever strength Craig's response possesses remains. Accordingly, I will narrow my discussion to what I see as the 'heart' of Craig's response to the soteriological challenge before us: his contention that all who are lost in this world suffer from transworld damnation. Or, to be more specific, I want to focus our discussion on what I will label the transworld damnation thesis (TDT):

> God would not have actualized this world if it contains anyone who does not respond positively to God under the circumstances encountered in this world but whose modal profile indicates would have responded positively to God under some other possible set of circumstances.

And the specific question I want to consider is whether a traditional exclusivist who affirms middle knowledge can justifiably utilize TDT as a response to the soteriological challenge at hand. In the same article to which I referred earlier, David Hunt argues that for the traditional exclusivist who is an Evangelical, the answer is clearly no. Evangelical traditional exclusivists such as Craig, Hunt points out, clearly believe that

(2) Christians must take every effort to communicate the life-giving message of salvation through Christ to those who are currently bound for hell.

But why are such Evangelicals so concerned? Why do they believe it is so important for Christians to share the gospel with the lost? The answer, as Hunt sees it, is obvious. They are assuming that

(3) Evangelistic efforts might make a difference in someone's salvation in the sense that it is possible that these efforts will result in someone's being saved who would not otherwise have been saved.

Given TDT, however, a person is damned only if she would not have responded to the gospel under any set of conceivable circumstances – including any set of circumstances in which any Christian might present the gospel to this person in this world. So contra (3), the fact that a traditional exclusivist fails to share the gospel with someone can never be a sufficient reason for someone's failure to respond positively to God and, therefore, for that person's eternal damnation. For, given TDT, if anyone who is lost *would have* responded to the gospel if it had been presented, then God would not have created this world – a world in which this person exists. And from this it obviously follows, Hunt points out, that evangelism is actually futile – that (2) cannot be affirmed consistently – given TDT.

Or, stated more informally, Hunt's argument is that a traditional exclusivist who affirms TDT cannot at the same time maintain justifiably that believers must make every effort to evangelize the lost since the very reason why such traditional exclusivists have historically thought it important to evangelize – their belief that some might be lost if they don't – no longer holds. Given transworld damnation, no one is ever lost because traditional exclusivists have actually failed to evangelize. They are lost, rather, because their modal profile indicates that they never would have accepted anyway, and this is something over which traditional exclusivists have absolutely no control.[36]

In one very important sense, Hunt is clearly right. If (3) – the belief that some might be lost because the gospel hasn't been shared with them – must be affirmed before a traditional exclusivist can in some meaningful sense affirm (2) – the contention that it is very important for Christians to share the gospel – then Hunt's criticism holds. For, given TDT – the contention that none are lost who would have accepted under any set of circumstances – (3) must be abandoned.

But, in fact, the relationship between (2) and (3) within Evangelical

Christianity is often not this clear-cut. It is true that Evangelical traditional exclusivists affirm (2): they do believe it is very important to share the gospel. It is also true that many Evangelicals at times affirm (3). But this is certainly not the case for all Evangelicals. To affirm (3) – to acknowledge that some might be lost because of what some Christian has failed to do – entails that God has voluntarily given over some control in the salvific arena to humans; that is it entails that in some cases it is we, not God, who can ultimately determine someone's eternal destiny. And even among Evangelical traditional exclusivists who are indeterminists – who believe that God cannot control the freely made decisions of any individual and thus cannot 'make' Christians freely share the gospel with someone – there continues to be the rather common belief that God will in some way make the gospel available to those who would have heard and accepted this salvific message if Christians hadn't 'fallen down on the job'.[37] Moreover, it seems to me that as long as these traditionalists are willing to acknowledge the direct divine intervention this perspective entails, they are justified in holding this position.

However, if an Evangelical traditional exclusivist rejects (3), how then can he or she affirm (2)? How can he or she take evangelism seriously? First, there has always been a very strong deontological (rule-based) perspective on evangelism in the traditional exclusivist community, even among those who are indeterminists. Specifically, it has long been held that Christians are not to obey God's commands primarily because they have come to understand why the command has been given. Rather, they are to do what God commands primarily because God has commanded it.[38]

Moreover, traditional exclusivists often maintain that even without (3), evangelism produces very beneficial consequences. Some, for example, point to the joy the believer can experience as the result of being used by God to accomplish his purposes. Or some, more privately, point to the possible negative consequences – for instance, the divine judgement – associated with not making themselves available to God for the working out of his salvific plan.

Now all this might seem very implausible to Hunt. Hunt appears to be a traditional exclusivist himself. And he may well believe personally that if (3) falls – if it isn't the case that some might be lost because Christians fail to evangelize – evangelism does become futile. However, this is beside the point. The criticism of TDT under consideration rests solely on Hunt's assumption that all, or at least the vast majority of, traditional exclusivists who believe that evangelism is not futile must be doing so because they affirm (3). However, this, as we have seen, need not be granted. Nor has Hunt demonstrated that traditional exclusivists must actually affirm (3) before (2) can be justifiably affirmed in any serious fashion. Thus, as things stand, the affirmation of TDT is only problematic for those traditional exclusivists who affirm middle knowledge and also actually do affirm (3) – also actually believe that their efforts determine the eternal destiny of some. And if forced to choose between the affirmation of (3) and a response to the soteriological challenge in question based on TDT, I believe that even some in this camp might opt for the latter.

Moreover, I can think of no other way in which it might be argued that a traditional exclusivist who affirms both middle knowledge and TDT is committed to a set of beliefs that are themselves inconsistent or incompatible with other essential traditional exclusivist beliefs. And thus it seems to me that the traditional exclusivist who affirms middle knowledge is justified in utilizing TDT to respond to the soteriological challenge at hand – to respond to the question of why an all-loving God would not ensure that all who are lost have heard the gospel – even if this traditional exclusivist is an Evangelical. This is not to say that I believe traditional exclusivists should affirm middle knowledge or that those who do must (or even should) utilize TDT as a response to the question at hand. However, I believe they are within their epistemic rights if they choose to do so.[39]

Is an appeal to TDT, though, a more plausible response to the question of 'eternal damnation' than that which can be offered by those traditional exclusivists such as Hunt who don't affirm middle knowledge? To answer this question, we must first identify more explicitly the type of response open to those exclusivists who reject middle knowledge. As has already been stated, all traditional exclusivists, regardless of what model of omniscience they affirm, can claim that those who don't hear the gospel in this life will be given an actual opportunity to accept Christ at death. However, what of those who believe that God does not possess middle knowledge and yet believe that one's eternal destiny is determined before death? If they also believe that many who never heard the gospel will spend eternity in hell, what type of response is available to them?

Many specific responses may be possible, but those of which I am aware contain the same basic line of reasoning. It is true, it is acknowledged, that since God does not possess middle knowledge, he did not know before the initiation of any given creative sequence who would or would not ultimately respond positively to God and thus ultimately spend eternity in heaven or hell. In this sense, creation was a risk. However, the inherent value of a world containing individuals with significant freedom – freedom that 'includes the potential for ... [both] the highest goods' and 'utterly damnable choices and actions' – outweighs this risk, especially since God is committed to doing all he can 'to defeat and redeem whatever evil might result'.[40]

Is this a viable response to the soteriological challenge in question? It is, I believe, a response that traditional exclusivists who reject middle knowledge can justifiably affirm. That is, I do not see that such a response is self-contradictory or incompatible with other basic traditional exclusivist tenets or can be shown on objective grounds to be false. And it seems to me to be just as plausible as the middle knowledge response affirmed by Craig, or any other middle knowledge response of which I can conceive. Is it, though, a more plausible response – or at least a less problematic response – than that which a traditional exclusivist who affirms middle knowledge can offer? Hunt, for one, thinks so. He sees any response incorporating middle knowledge as 'more of a challenge to God's omnibenevolence than the scenario of a risky creation undertaken by a God prepared to defeat and redeem whatever evil might result'.[41]

However, Hunt's comparative assessment strikes me as dubious. If, as Hunt acknowledges, a God without middle knowledge did not know before creation if any who will not respond positively in this world would have responded positively under any other conceivable circumstances, then it is possible that some (or many) in this world are lost who would have accepted God if things had been different – if, for example, God had initiated a different world. But if this is so, then at creation a God without middle knowledge was taking a very serious risk indeed, a risk that may result in much eternal suffering that will not be 'defeated and redeemed'. And to posit that an all-loving God – especially one who has an *a priori* commitment to allowing individuals to go to hell under certain conditions – would gamble in this way seems to me to be no less serious a difficulty than any faced by a traditional exclusivist who believes God possesses middle knowledge and affirms a soteriological theodicy based on something such as TDT.[42]

Conclusion

Where does all this leave us? The central question under discussion is whether traditional exclusivists can justifiably claim that many, if not most, non-Christians will spend eternity separated from God. What we should conclude, I have argued, is that while both those traditional exclusivists who believe God possesses middle knowledge and those who don't can justifiably affirm responses to the problem of 'eternal damnation' that cannot be demonstrated on objective grounds to be inadequate, those in neither camp have demonstrated in any objective, non-question-begging sense that their response is more adequate than the other.

Our extended discussion of this soteriological issue also illustrates at least two important points I have attempted to highlight in previous chapters. First, it illustrates that epistemic peer conflict over a religious issue is just as likely to exist among proponents of the same basic theistic system as among proponents of differing basic theistic systems – that significant diversity of religious thought (even with respect to the same issue) is just as likely to exist at the intra-system level as the inter-system level. In fact, this discussion highlights the fact that contemporary philosophical discussions of religious concepts (whether the issue be evil or miracles or God's power or knowledge) are often more likely to center on disputes within basic systems than disputes among basic theistic systems.

Accordingly, this discussion also illustrates well the inadequacy of defining exclusivism in terms of allegiance to a basic theistic system (one world religion) since all Christians, regardless of their actual soteriological perspective, are exclusivists in this sense. It illustrates that if we desire a comprehensive assessment of exclusivistic belief, we need to maintain, as noted in Chapter 1, that a person is a religious exclusivist not only when she believes the doctrinal perspective of only one basic theistic system (for instance, only one of the major world religions) to be true, but also when she believes only one of the doctrinal variants within a basic theistic system (for instance, Christianity) to be the truth or closer to the truth than any other doctrinal perspective on this issue.

Notes

1. As noted in Chapter 1 (note 1), since most philosophers use 'religious diversity' to label the type of epistemic tension with which this book is concerned, I normally do so also.
2. Process theist Charles Hartshorne, for instance, considers belief in immortality to be a 'tall story' concocted by those who have not yet realized that 'the world is not a kindergarten' in which all our wishes are granted. See *Omnipotence and Other Theological Mistakes* (Albany, NY, SUNY Press, 1984), pp. 36–7. For a good discussion of the annihilation theory, see David L. Edwards and John Stott, *Evangelical Essentials* (Downers Grove, IL: InterVarsity Press, 1988), pp. 287–329.
3. Richard Swinburne, *Responsibility and Atonement* (Oxford: Clarendon Press, 1989), p. 182.
4. For a good discussion of the history of Universalism in the United States, see Ernest Cassara, ed., *Universalism in America*, (Boston: Beacon Press, 1971).
5. A fuller discussion of Hick's version of this criticism can be found in Chapter 4.
6. See, for example, John Sanders, ed., *What about Those Who Have Never Heard?: Three Views on the Destiny of the Unevangelized* (Downers Grove, IL: InterVarsity Press, 1995).
7. A fuller discussion of this point can be found in David Basinger, *The Case For Freewill Theism* (Downers Grove, IL: InterVarsity Press, 1996), Chapter 3.
8. R.B. Kuiper in *The Voice of Authority*, G.W. Marston, ed. (Philadelphia: Presbyterian and Reformed Publishing House, 1960), p. 16.
9. See Gottfried Leibniz, excerpts from *Theodicy* in William Rowe and William Wainwright, *Philosophy and Religion: Selected Readings*, 2nd edn (New York: Harcourt, Brace, Jovanovich, 1987), especially pp. 203–205.
10. See, for instance, Norman Geisler, *The Christian Ethic of Love* (Grand Rapids, MI: Zondervan, 1973), pp. 21–5.
11. Ibid., p. 22.
12. I am here using the term 'children' in reference to those of any chronological age who do not have the mental capacity to make the decision in question. 'Adults' are those of any age who do.
13. See Samuel Barrows, *The Doom of the Majority of Mankind* (Boston: American Unitarian Association, 1883), pp. 26–38 for an interesting presentation of these perspectives.
14. Even Samuel Barrows, writing a century ago, could state that 'modern Calvinists, repudiating the doctrine of infant damnation, would like to believe that all dying in infancy are elect'. (Barrows, p. 37), Also, see Neal Punt, *What's So Good About the Good News?* (Chicago: Northland Press, 1988), pp. 65–9 for a thoughtful current defence of the claim that all young children who die enter heaven.
15. See, for example, Dick Dowsett, *God, That's Not Fair!* (Kent, UK: OMF Books, 1982), pp. 31–52; Punt, pp. 13–19.
16. See Michael Paternoster, *Thou Art There Also: God, Death and Hell* (London: SPCK, 1967) for a good historical survey of this doctrine. Also see Punt, pp.19–25. Not all traditionalist exclusivists, however, accept this contention. One current Evangelical manifesto declares that 'all men have some knowledge of God through his general revelation, [but] we deny this can save', Edwards and Stott, p. 287.

17. See, for instance, Punt, pp. 93–101.
18. Ibid., p. 95.
19. Jonathan Kvanvig, *The Problem of Hell* (New York: Oxford University Press, 1993), pp. 152, 155.
20. See, for instance Punt, p. 66; Edwards and Stott, p. 326.
21. For a more in-depth discussion of the models of omniscience to follow, see William Hasker, *God, Time and Knowledge* (Ithaca: Cornell University Press, 1989), pp. 19–63.
22. Traditionalists, remember, are indeterminists.
23. David P. Hunt, 'Middle Knowledge and the Soteriological Problem of Evil', *Religious Studies* 27 (March 1991), pp. 3–26.
24. Ibid., p. 18.
25. Ibid., p. 22.
26. Ibid., p. 20.
27. Ibid., p. 22.
28. Ibid., p. 19.
29. Ibid., p. 24.
30. William Lane Craig, *The Only Wise God* (Grand Rapids, MI: Baker Book House, 1987), pp. 145–51; '"No Other Name": A Middle Knowledge Perspective on the Exclusivity of Salvation Through Christ', *Faith and Philosophy*, 6 (April, 1989), pp. 172–88.
31. Craig, *The Only Wise God*, p. 147.
32. Craig, *Faith and Philosophy*, p. 184.
33. Ibid., pp. 184–5.
34. Ibid., p. 186.
35. Craig, *The Only Wise God*, p. 148.
36. Hunt, pp. 12–18.
37. Of course, theological determinists who believe that God can unilaterally control human choice must reject (3), that is, must deny that God's salvific control is limited in this fashion.
38. See, for example, J.I. Packer, *Evangelism and the Sovereignty of God* (Downers Grove, IL: InterVarsity Press, 1961).
39. See David Basinger, 'Practical Implications', *The Openness of God* (Downers Grove, IL: InterVarsity Press, 1994), pp. 155–76.
40. Michael Peterson, *Evil and the Christian God* (Grand Rapids, MI: Baker Book House, 1982), p. 104; Hunt, p. 26.
41. Hunt, p. 26.
42. Much of material in this chapter first appeared (in slightly different form) in 'Divine Omniscience and the Soteriological Problem of Evil: Is the Type of Knowledge God Possesses Relevant?' *Religious Studies* 28 (1991), pp. 1–18. Used with permission.

Chapter 6

Diversity and Positive Apologetics

While most pluralists, including Hick, openly attempt to convince others to adopt their positions on religious diversity (epistemic peer conflict)[1], the philosophical exclusivists we have been considering tend to be more defensive. That is, rather than arguing that all should affirm some form of exclusivism, they primarily defend the epistemic right of the exclusivist to retain her exclusivity in the face of such diversity. They engage, in other words, primarily in what has been labelled *negative apologetics*.

However, many, if not most, practicing exclusivists do not stop there. They, like most pluralists, try to convince others that they are right. That is, like most pluralists, they engage in what has come to be labelled *positive apologetics*. But is an exclusivist justified in engaging in this activity? And if so, is she obligated to do so? These are the questions with which this chapter is concerned.

Clarification of Key Terms

For the purpose of this discussion, it is important that we have a clearer understanding of the relevant terminology. As I will be using the phrase, for someone to engage in *negative apologetics* with respect to a specific religious belief is for her to defend her right to hold this belief justifiably by defeating or fending off potential defeaters, while for someone to engage in what I will label *positive apologetics* is for her to offer, or at least attempt to identify, sufficient reasons for considering a specific religious belief to be superior to competing beliefs. Such 'positive' reasons might include standard propositional arguments designed to demonstrate that the belief in question is true or at least the most plausible of the alternatives.[2] However, such reasons need not include any form of propositional argumentation at all. For instance, for a person to maintain simply that she finds a specific religious belief the best (most convincing or reasonable or plausible) among the self-consistent options would be, for our purposes, for her to offer a reason for its affirmation and thus to engage in positive apologetics.[3]

I also want to distinguish between two forms of positive apologetics. For someone to engage in what will be labelled *personal positive apologetics* is for her to attempt to identify, for her own benefit, what she considers to be sufficient reasons for holding a certain belief – for maintaining that this belief is superior to all competing beliefs.[4] For someone to engage in what will be labelled *proselytizing positive apologetics* is for her to offer reasons for the affirmation of a specific religious belief to someone who does not presently affirm this belief – is for her to offer reasons for someone else to convert to her perspective.

This latter form of positive apologetics can, of course, be related to personal positive apologetics in many ways. An exclusivist engaging in personal positive apologetics – attempting to identify positive reasons for the affirmation of a given belief for her own benefit – might become convinced, or simply finds herself believing, that she should share these reasons with others – that she should engage in proselytizing positive apologetics. And it may well be that the process used to attempt to discover positive reasons to retain a specific religious belief will be exactly the same, and produce the same results, as the process used to attempt to discover positive reasons that can be used to convince others to affirm this belief. The conceptual difference between the two types of positive apologetics, as I am defining them, has to do with the primary motivation for each. A person engages in personal positive apologetics primarily for her own sake; a person engages in proselytizing positive apologetics primarily for the sake of others.

To help make these distinctions a little more tangible, let us apply them to a hypothetical discussion concerning the nature of God's power. Sue, let us assume, believes that God has unilateral control over all states of affairs, including free human choice, while Bill holds that to the extent God grants humans freedom, God voluntarily gives up control over that which is chosen. If, in response to Sue's claim that his position is unbiblical or incompatible with a meaningful concept of the greatest possible being or posits a being not 'strong' enough to be worthy of worship, Bill argues that Sue cannot demonstrate objectively (in any non-question-begging form) that any of this is true and that he is for this reason justified in continuing to hold his belief, he has engaged in negative apologetics. If Bill, in response to Sue's challenge, considers or reconsiders his own reasons for believing his perspective to be superior to that offered by Sue in an attempt to assure himself that his perspective is indeed superior, he has engaged in personal positive apologetics. And, finally, if he attempts to convince Sue to accept his perspective, he has engaged in proselytizing positive apologetics.

Negative Apologetics

With these clarifications in mind, let us now consider the question of whether apologetical activity is justified and, if so, should be considered an obligation. With respect to negative apologetics, Reformed Epistemologists, as we have seen, believe not only that this form of apologetics is a justifiable activity but also that it is a requirement – that the exclusivist is required to attempt to defeat potential defeaters of her exclusivistic belief. As they see it, remember, to fulfil this obligation, it is not necessary for the exclusivist to produce reasons for the affirmation of the belief in question that are convincing to all. To retain justified belief, the exclusivist need only defend herself against the claim that her belief is self-contradictory, incompatible with other firmly held beliefs, or empirically false. But some such defence – some such form of negative apologetics – is considered necessary.

While almost all exclusivists, whether or not they are Reformed Epistemologists, agree that to engage in negative apologetics in this sense is an epistemic duty, some do not. Specifically, those sometimes labelled *paradox theists* believe that while God's truth cannot actually be self-contradictory, such truth may at times appear so from a human perspective. In fact, they hold that some truth will never appear self-consistent 'before the bar of human reason'.[5] Consequently, they see little need to engage in even negative apologetics to retain justified belief.

However, as I have argued in other contexts, paradox theism does not appear to be a coherent theological perspective.[6] So I agree with the vast majority of exclusivists that, when faced with diversity of religious thought, the form of negative apologetics in question is necessary.

Personal Positive Apologetics

How, though, ought the exclusivist to view positive apologetics? Can she justifiably engage in this activity, and, if so, ought she do so? Turning first to personal positive apologetics – to attempts to identify for oneself sufficient reasons for continued belief – while no one claims that exclusivists cannot justifiably engage in this form of apologetic activity,[7] a number of exclusivists deny that they need necessarily do so to retain justified belief.

Alvin Plantinga, for instance, certainly believes that an exclusivist can justifiably engage in personal positive apologetics. As we saw in Chapter 4, he acknowledges that 'for many or most exclusivists ... an awareness of the enormous variety of human religious response serves as ... an *undercutting* defeater' in the sense that 'it directly reduces [their] level of confidence or degree of belief'. In fact, he believes that 'since degree of warrant depends in part on degree of belief, it is possible, though not necessary, that knowledge of the facts of religious pluralism should reduce an exclusivist's degree of belief and hence warrant ... in such a way as to deprive him of knowledge'.[8] And for those in this position, Plantinga grants that the consideration of supporting reasons for continued affirmation may be in order. Yet he clearly does not believe that to engage in this form of personal apologetics is an obligation. It is rather an option for those who find the reality of religious diversity a significant challenge to continued exclusivistic commitment.[9]

I obviously disagree. Throughout this book, I have argued that if an exclusivist wants to maximize truth (wants to minimize error), then, in the face of diversity (when faced with true epistemic peer conflict), she is obligated to attempt to identify and assess the reasons why she and her competitors hold the beliefs they do. And this, as I see it, is simply another way of saying that she needs to search for reasons for continuing to consider her perspective superior to that of her epistemic competitors – that she is obligated to engage in personal positive apologetics.

Or, stated differently yet, it is my contention, in contrast with what Plantinga believes, that when an exclusivist finds herself facing epistemic peer conflict – when she finds herself affirming a perspective that is rejected by other seemingly sincere, knowledgeable individuals – she is obligated to engage in personal positive apologetics, even if she does not find such conflict troubling personally. At the very least, to follow on a theme first introduced in Chapter 2, to engage in such apologetical activity is, I maintain, a very good idea.

Proselytizing Positive Apologetics

What, though, of proselytizing positive apologetics? Can the exclusivist justifiably attempt to convert others to her perspective and, if so, ought she do so?

Most non-exclusivists who believe the answer to be no – who believe such proselytization is not justified – challenge the moral character of the exclusivist who attempts to convince those with whom she differs to accept her perspective alone as the truth. For instance, Wilfred Cantwell Smith argues that 'except at the cost of insensitivity or delinquency, it is morally not possible actually to go out into the world and say to devout, intelligent fellow human beings [that] we believe that we know God and we are right; you believe that you know God, and you are totally wrong'.[10] And when Joseph Runzo claims that exclusivism can be 'highly presumptive' and 'morally repugnant',[11] or Hick maintains that exclusivists often manifest a sort of arbitrariness or arrogance[12] or harmful 'natural pride',[13] they too appear to be challenging the moral character of those who attempt to convert others to their perspectives.

However, why exactly should it be considered insensitive or arrogant or presumptive for an exclusivist to attempt to convince others that her perspective is the correct one – to tell others that she is right and they are wrong? Of course, if an exclusivist had to acknowledge (were forced to acknowledge) that her position was unjustifiable or at least extremely implausible (even if not unjustified), then it might well be true that for her then to attempt to convert others to her position would be morally inappropriate. However, as we have seen in previous chapters, not only can the exclusivist justifiably maintain that her perspective is superior (as even Hick admits),[14] she can, in fact, justifiably maintain that her perspective is as plausible as any alternative. And if someone justifiably believes her position to be plausible, it is difficult to see how her attempt to convince others they should agree can be considered arrogant or presumptive or insensitive, especially if she believes that it is important for the welfare of those she is attempting to convert that they do so.

Moreover, while it is surely true that some conversion is attempted for what we would all agree are morally inappropriate reasons – for instance, for financial gain or to gain power over others – there is little empirical evidence that exclusivists in general have these motives. It is probably true, rather, that many, if not most, exclusivists who proselytize do so primarily because they believe they have what others need and are willing (sometimes at great personal cost) to share it with them.

Finally, even if it could be shown that those exclusivists wanting to proselytize are doing so for what we all consider to be dubious, even highly offensive reasons, this wouldn't demonstrate that proselytizing, itself, is inherently problematic.

There is, though, another, more interesting way in which the moral appropriateness of proselytizing exclusivistic activity might be challenged. It may well be true, the critic might admit, that if an exclusivist really believed that the epistemic superiority of her perspective could be demonstrated objectively, she would then be morally justified in trying (perhaps even obligated to try) to convert those who disagreed, especially if she thought that such a conversion would be in the best interest of the potential convert.

However, the critic might continue, even most exclusivists agree that we are not in this position with respect to many religious issues. That is, most exclusivists agree that with respect to many, if not most, significant religious issues on which there is disagreement, objective adjudication is not at present possible. In fact, it is for this reason that most exclusivists acknowledge that those with whom they disagree are justified in holding opposing perspectives. However, if an exclusivist must acknowledge not only that she cannot demonstrate her perspective to be epistemically superior, but also that those holding opposing perspectives are as justified in holding theirs as she is in holding hers, is it not morally presumptuous or insensitive or arrogant for her to attempt to convince them to convert to her position?

Again, I think the answer is no. It may well be that the realization that her epistemic opponents are equally justified in holding incompatible perspectives on debated issues will affect an exclusivist's personal desire to convince these competitors to agree with her perspective. However, for an exclusivist to acknowledge that her epistemic opponents are justified in their beliefs is not incompatible with believing firmly that her own position is the correct one. And as long as this latter belief is present, then I don't see how it can be argued that an exclusivist desiring to convince others to see it her way is acting, in principle, in a presumptuous, insensitive manner, even if she does realize that those she is attempting to convert can justifiably retain their current perspectives.

Perhaps, though, the critic will persist. With respect to the transformational power of religious commitment, most exclusivists, as we have seen, acknowledge that there is no way to demonstrate objectively that one religious perspective has, in principle, greater transformational efficacy than do the others.[15] However, if this is so, that is, if an exclusivist acknowledges that other perspectives are equally efficacious, then what right, it might be argued, does she have to try to convince proponents of these other perspectives to switch to hers?

This challenge, though, is based on a confusion that has already been noted in an earlier chapter but needs to be revisited more thoroughly in this context.[16] It is crucial that we distinguish between the claim that

(1) There is no objective basis upon which it can be demonstrated that any given religious perspective has greater transformational efficacy (or more salvific power) than competing perspectives,

and the claim that

(2) The exclusivist cannot justifiably maintain that her religious perspective has greater transformational efficacy (or more salvific power) than competing perspectives.

If (2) were true, then it would, I believe, be debatable whether proselytizing was appropriate. That is, if someone really did believe that switching to her perspective would make no practical difference in the lives of those she is attempting to convert, then the question of whether proselytizing is a justifiable activity does at the very least become open to serious discussion. However, it is at this point that earlier comments by Kelly Clarke become relevant. As he has argued (I think correctly), even if (1) is true – even if there exists no objective basis on which it can be established that one perspective has greater transformational efficacy – it does not follow that an exclusivist cannot continue to maintain justifiably that her perspective does in fact have more transformational efficacy – cannot justifiably continue to reject (2). And as long as an exclusivist can justifiably deny (2) – can justifiably maintain that her perspective does have superior transformational efficacy – the fact that she also admits that she cannot objectively demonstrate this to be so does not, it seems to me, count against the moral appropriateness of any proselytizing effort.[17]

Accordingly, I think we must conclude that there exists no sound epistemic or experiential basis on which to argue that an exclusivist cannot justifiably engage in proselytizing activity, or even that such activity ought to be considered morally suspect.

What, though, of the much stronger claim: that an exclusivist ought to engage in proselytizing activity, that it is an obligation for the exclusivist to do so? While few philosophers, even those who are the strongest defenders of exclusivism, have wanted to claim there is such an obligation, Paul Griffith does offer a qualified argument to this end. Specifically, he sets forth and defends what he identifies as the 'principle of the necessity of inter-religious apologetics (the NOIA principle)':

For any two religious communities, R1 and R2, any two ordered sets of sentences, S1 and S2, and any time, T: If S1 and S2 are doctrines of R1 and R2, and if, at T, representative intellectuals of R1 come to judge that some members of S2 are incompatible with some members of S1 (or that S2 and S1 *in toto* are incompatible), then the representative intellectuals in question should feel obliged to engage in both positive and negative apologetics *vis-à-vis* S2.[18]

It is most important to emphasize initially that Griffith is not claiming that 'every member of a religious community who finds herself in the situation described by the NOIA principle is thereby required to engage in apologetics'. It is his contention, rather, 'only that every community should have some individuals among its members who respond this way'.[19]

Exactly why, though, is the community obligated to engage in proselytizing activity of this form?[20] The most important reason, we are told, is because religious communities are formed around the belief that certain doctrines are true, and that it is therefore 'part of their epistemic duty to consider whether a challenging sentence or set of such makes it improper to continue asserting what the community asserts'. And while such an effort, Griffith acknowledges, often initially involves some form of negative apologetics, 'it may often (and should) pass from there into positive apologetics – the attempt to show not only that the attack fails, but that the doctrines of the community being attacked are cognitively superior'.[21]

Furthermore, Griffith adds, there is for many religious communities an ethical reason to engage in proselytizing activity. Since 'it is beyond doubt that virtually all religious communities assert that there is some ... relation between assent to some set of doctrine-expressing sentences and the attainment of salvation', then, for those communities who also believe that the 'salvation of non-members is important ... [t]he conclusion that there is thus an ethical imperative placed upon such communities to engage in positive apologetics is therefore at least suggested'.[22]

While I am in agreement with much of what Griffith says, I think that in the final analysis his contention that all exclusivistic communities are obligated to engage in positive proselytizing apologetics is simply too strong.

Let us first consider Griffith's epistemic contention: that in the face of religious diversity – when faced with incompatible doctrinal claims made by seemingly knowledgeable, sincere members of other religious communities – a religious community has an epistemic duty to consider whether it is 'improper to continue asserting what the community asserts', and that this should involve an 'attempt to show not only that the attack fails, but that the doctrines of the community being attacked are cognitively superior'.

Not surprisingly, I agree completely with Griffith's claim that a religious community has an epistemic obligation to assess incompatible claims offered by seemingly knowledgeable, sincere members of other religious communities, as this is simply another version of Basinger's Rule. Moreover, I agree that such belief assessment does often 'pass from there into positive [proselytizing] apologetics'. In fact, I'm willing to grant for the sake of argument that within those communities in which there is an internal doctrinal mandate to 'share' the truth, proponents should feel an obligation to do so. But it does not in any obvious sense follow from this that NOIA is true – that all religious communities involved in belief assessment should, even in the absence of any relevant internal requirement, engage in proselytizing activity. And Griffith, as far as I can see, offers us no explicit argument for this stronger contention.

There is, though, an available argument for this stronger claim. One of the basic assumptions of this book is that most of us rightly feel some obligation to maximize truth. However, it might be argued, for those desiring to maximize truth (especially those who are 'intellectuals'), there is an epistemic obligation not only to attempt to resolve epistemic peer conflict for one's own personal benefit, but also an inherent obligation to *share* the results with others, even if there is no obvious practical value in doing so or no internal doctrinal mandate that this be done. For instance, with respect to the question of how one attains salvation, it might be argued that quite apart from any ethical concern about the welfare of others or any internal requirement to attempt to convert others, the fact that an exclusivist desires to maximize truth means that she is obligated not only to defend her perspective – engage in negative apologetics – but also to attempt to convince others that she is right.

I agree in part with this general line of reasoning. It seems to me that if someone has knowledge of a line of reasoning that will resolve an epistemic conflict conclusively, then she may well be under an obligation to share this information with those who don't agree, even if there is no obvious practical value or relevant mandate.

However, most philosophers, as I have repeatedly noted, believe that with respect to many, if not most disputed religious issues, there exists (at least at present) no non-question-begging form of resolution. And in the absence of objective resolution – in a context where those on both sides can justifiably retain their positions – it isn't at all clear to me that there exists any general epistemic obligation to attempt to convince one's epistemic competitors that one's perspective is superior, even if one does desire to maximize truth.

Moreover, to return to a more general assessment of NOIA, not only do not all exclusivistic systems mandate or even encourage proselytizing activity, within some religious communities (for instance, within some forms of Judaism) proselytization is discouraged. And for proponents of these communities, it isn't only the case that they need not engage in proselytization of the type in question they cannot justifiably do so, given the core beliefs of the exclusivistic system they affirm.[23]

So we must conclude, I believe, that Griffith's epistemic support for NOIA – for the claim that all religious communities must engage in positive proselytizing apologetics – is inadequate.

This still leaves us, though, with Griffith's ethical support for NOIA: his claim that for those religious communities in which it is held that the salvation of non-members is important, there exists an ethical imperative to proselytize. I've already stated that I believe this to be correct. But since, as Griffith himself acknowledges, not all religious communities do hold that the salvation of non-members is important, it is obvious that this ethical argument is not support for the strong version of NOIA, that is, for the claim that *all* religious communities should engage in proselytization.

There may well be, though, a somewhat related ethical obligation that does hold for all religious communities. It is true (as far as I know) that all religious communities affirm doctrines believed to have very significant practical benefits for our lives. That is, within all such communities it is held that to engage or refrain from engaging in certain practices – for instance, to forgive those who have wronged you, to live for a purpose outside of yourself, to abstain from overindulgence in food or drink – will lead to the most satisfying, meaningful life possible. Hence, since I believe that all of us are under a basic ethical obligation to help others experience a satisfying life, I do believe that those in all religious communities are under a *prima facie* obligation to share even with non-members what they see as the 'path to personal fulfillment'.

However, this is not necessarily support for the strong version of NOIA since the proponent of a specific religious perspective may be able to acknowledge an obligation to be concerned about the welfare of others without needing also to acknowledge an obligation to attempt to convert them to her religious perspective. It is only if the doctrines of a specific religious community stipulate conversion (stipulate acceptance of the basic doctrines of that system) as a necessary condition for a satisfying life that an obligation to proselytize would hold. And not all religious communities believe this to be so.

In short, it appears that whether our considerations are epistemic or ethical, it cannot be argued that all exclusivists (or even some individuals from each exclusivistic community) are required to engage in proselytizing activity. Rather, whether such activity is a requirement for any given exclusivist depends on whether the core beliefs of the basic theistic system to which this exclusivist is committed mandate that she attempts to convert others.

Before concluding this chapter, however, I want to explore some epistemic tensions that diversity might pose for those exclusivists who are required, or simply desire, to proselytize.

The first, and most obvious, tension arises in relation to Alston's claim that an exclusivist should, in the face of unresolved epistemic peer conflict, simply sit tight with the perspective she holds.[24] Let us assume, for instance, that Jim, an exclusivist, is convinced by Alston that he should, in the face of unresolved conflict, remain committed to the religious perspective he currently affirms. However, let us further assume that what Jim currently believes is not only that those who don't hold his perspective – don't affirm the beliefs of his theological system and engage in its practices – are missing the peace and joy they could be experiencing now, but that they are also in danger of spending eternity separated from God. Finally, let us assume that because he believes his basic theistic system requires that he care for the well-being of others, Jim also believes he is under a mandate to proselytize – to try to convert others to his perspective.

If Jim, in acting out this mandate, approaches an individual who currently affirms no competing religious perspective, then Alston's suggestion that a person sit tight with her current religious perspective has, of course, little bearing. However, Jim may well be trying to convert others who hold religious perspectives incompatible with his own. If he is a Christian, for instance, he may well be trying to convert a Muslim so that this person, too, can spend eternity with God. And here Alston's suggestion that an exclusivist sit tight, if accepted by Jim as a good basis for justifiably retaining his exclusivistic belief in the face of diversity, does, it seems to me, generate at least a *prima facie* epistemic tension.

Alston's contention that an exclusivist sit tight, remember, is not intended to support the exclusivity of any specific religious perspective. His claim is that all parties in an epistemic dispute that cannot be resolved conclusively should retain their current perspectives. With respect to the question of one's eternal destiny, for instance, Alston's 'sit tight' policy applies not only to those who believe that only Christians can spend eternity with God but also to those who believe that only true Muslims can do so. Hence, if Jim retains his exclusivity on the basis of Alston's argument – if Jim retains his exclusivistic position on the eternal destiny of humankind because he agrees that a theist ought to sit tight in the face of unresolved epistemic conflict – then he must also maintain that his competitors ought to sit tight for the same reason. However, if this is so, then Jim appears to be in the awkward position of believing simultaneously that it is important that those with whom he disagrees convert to his perspective but also that they should not do so – should instead sit tight with what they have. That is, it appears that Jim's affirmation of Alston's 'sit tight' policy places him in the troubling epistemic position of believing both that he should attempt to convert his competitors and that he should not do so.

It is important to keep in mind, however, that a proselytizing exclusivist need not, as I see it, face this tension. As I argued earlier in relation to Alston, while an exclusivist can decide justifiably to remain committed to what she currently believes in the face of epistemic peer conflict, I don't believe she need do so. She can, as the result of the belief assessment I claim such conflict requires, also justifiably decide to switch to another basic theistic perspective or suspend judgement. And, of course, for the exclusivist who views peer conflict in this manner, proselytization is no longer inherently problematic.

There still remains, though, one aspect of the relationship between diversity and positive proselytizing apologetics yet to be explored, namely the relationship between degree of conviction and apologetic motivation. Most philosophers acknowledge that belief is not an 'all or nothing' state of affairs. Specifically, belief admits to degrees of conviction or confidence with respect to both truth and practical significance.

Let us assume, for instance, that Sue, Pete, Sally and Ted all believe that a given candidate, Mary, is the best of those running for a political office. The fact that they all believe this to be true in no sense entails that they hold this belief with equal conviction or that they agree on the practical significance of the election. Sue might believe with absolute conviction not only that Mary is the only qualified candidate but also that the person elected will have the opportunity to enact meaningful change. Pete might also believe with absolute conviction that Mary is the only qualified candidate but be much less certain that meaningful change is possible, even if Mary is elected. Sally might find herself barely convinced that Mary is the best of a number of highly qualified candidates, but believes quite firmly that the person elected will be in a position to enact meaningful change. Ted might also find himself barely convinced that Mary is the best of a number of highly qualified candidates and be quite uncertain that change is likely to occur, regardless of who is elected.

Moreover, it is quite likely that, if these individuals did have these differing 'levels of conviction', it would have a significant impact on the relevant political activity of the individuals in question. For instance, since neither Pete nor Ted is firmly convinced that the election will be of much practical consequence, neither is very likely to volunteer to work as a member of Mary's campaign committee. On the other hand, given Sally's belief in the significance of the election, she might become a member of Mary's committee, even though she is not firmly convinced Mary is the best candidate. And Sue is quite likely to become involved, given that she strongly believes not only that Mary is the only qualified candidate but that the person elected will be in a position to make a difference.

The same sort of 'degree of conviction' distinctions can also be applied to religious issues. It is possible for a given set of individuals to agree, for instance, that the Christian God exists or that only Muslims will be in heaven or that God does not have exhaustive knowledge of the future or that God did not create men and women with inherent differences relevant to leadership, and yet hold the belief in question with quite differing degrees of conviction with respect to truth or relevance. Confidence that the belief is true could run all the way from the unwavering conviction that this perspective on the issue is the only option with any rational support to the rather tepid acknowledgement that this perspective seems only slightly more plausible than other plausible perspectives. And the perceived significance could run all the way from the firm conviction that the response to no issue could have greater practical impact to the firm conviction that there is very little of practical value at stake.

Moreover, these differing degrees of conviction may well result in differing degrees of desire to proselytize. If the proponent of a given perspective on a religious issue believes that her position is clearly the most reasonable and also believes passionately that the issue is of great significance, then she is very likely to find herself highly motivated to 'share this truth' with others. On the other hand, if she doesn't believe that her perspective is significantly more reasonable than other options and/or doesn't believe that the issue is of great significance, then she will be much less likely to find herself with the desire to 'convert' others to her position.

If a Christian, for instance, is clearly convinced that only those who 'accept Christ' will spend eternity with God and feels that there is nothing more important than one's eternal destiny, then she will quite likely find herself with the strong desire to 'share the good news of Christ' with others. However, if she finds the contention that one must 'accept Christ' to spend eternity with God only slightly more plausible than the contention that all who sincerely commit themselves to God, as they conceive of him, will enter God's kingdom, or if she really believes that we ought to concentrate our efforts on making our earthly lives as meaningful as possible and isn't strongly convinced that 'commitment to Christ' is the only way to experience such meaning, then she will quite likely not find herself with a strong desire to convert others to her Christian position.

It is here where the reality of diversity can come directly into play. As most philosophers, including those defending exclusivism, acknowledge, the fact that many, many seemingly sincere, knowledgeable individuals are firmly committed to incompatible religious perspectives can (and probably does) negatively affect the degree of conviction with which some exclusivists hold their religious perspectives to be superior.[25] And the seeming transformational parity of the various basic religious systems can (and probably does) diminish for some exclusivists the perceived practical significance of affirming the superiority of their specific religious systems. Hence, if it is true, as I am arguing, that one's desire to proselytize is tied in some meaningful sense to one's level of confidence in the truth and/or perceived significance of that which is to be shared with others, it seems reasonable to conclude that awareness of religious diversity probably does have a significant negative impact on the desire of at least some exclusivists to proselytize.

However, I doubt that this negative impact is as widespread as it might appear it would be. As I see it, what usually does actually diminish an exclusivist's confidence in a religious belief, to the extent that this occurs, is not simply awareness of seeming transformational parity or of the fact that seemingly sincere, knowledgeable individuals affirm incompatible perspectives on important religious issues. As I see it, exclusivists normally begin to experience less confidence in their exclusivistic beliefs only when they find themselves forced to acknowledge personally that those with whom they disagree really are on equal transformational or epistemic footing. However, many exclusivists, as we have seen, do not really believe that such parity actually exists. Many believe (justifiably), rather, that they are in a superior position. And as long as exclusivists do not actually acknowledge such parity, there is little reason to believe that awareness of religious diversity will have much effect on their degree of personal conviction and thus their desire to proselytize.[26]

Moreover, we must keep in mind that even for some of those exclusivists whose *desire* to proselytize has been diminished by the reality of diversity, the actual extent to which they proselytize may in fact be little affected. It might well be that the primary reason for their proselytizing activity is the fact that their basic theistic system dictates that they ought to do so, regardless of how they 'feel' about it or how significant they believe the intended result. Or it could be that even if their basic system does not require that they proselytize, the desire of these exclusivists to please God or demonstrate their spirituality by proselytizing outweighs whatever degree of negative impact their awareness of religious diversity has had on their desire to 'share the truth'.

Still, it should be noted that awareness of religious diversity could negatively impact, in an indirect manner, the proselytizing activity of even this group of exclusivists. To the extent that exclusivists heed Basinger's Rule, their awareness of religious diversity will lead to belief assessment, and such assessment, I have argued, can lead to thinner theologies – theologies that are less incompatible with competing theologies than before. And the thinner the theology of an exclusivist, the fewer individuals there may be to convert and the less there may be to convert them to.

Conclusion

The central question of this chapter is whether the exclusivist can justifiably engage in apologetic activity, and if so, whether she is obligated to do so. With respect to negative apologetics – the attempt by an exclusivist to defend the right to her exclusivity in the face of diversity – I have argued not only that an exclusivist can justifiably defend her exclusivity but that she is obligated to do so – is obligated to attempt to defeat potential defeaters.

With respect to personal positive apologetics – the attempt by an exclusivist to identify for herself what she considers to be sufficient reasons for retaining an exclusivist perspective – I have argued that, when encountering diversity, an exclusivist not only can justifiably engage in this form of apologetic activity, she is obligated by Basinger's Rule to do so.

Finally, with respect to proselytizing positive apologetics – the attempt by an exclusivist to convert others to her perspective – I have argued that while proselytization is justifiable, and can even be considered obligatory by the exclusivist whose basic theistic system requires such activity, it cannot be argued that all exclusivists are under an obligation to attempt to convince others to agree.

Notes

1. While in previous chapters I couched my discussion primarily in terms of either 'religious diversity' or 'epistemic peer conflict', the nature and specific content of this chapter dictate that both descriptors appear frequently. (Cf. Chapter 1, note 1.)
2. That is, as I will be using this phrase, positive apologetics is not synonymous with Evidentialism – the offering of positive evidence for a belief.
3. I recognize that the line between negative and positive apologetics, thus defined, is quite fuzzy. There is a certain sense, for instance, in which the ability to fend off a critic's attack becomes (or can become) a reason to continue to affirm a given belief, and a sense in which an argument for one's position is a defence against attack. But there surely is a meaningful distinction between defending what one believes and identifying the reasons for affirming what one wants to defend, and it is to this distinction that I wish to point.
4. It is also possible for this form of positive apologetics to be a group activity. That is, sometimes a group of individuals who share the same basic religious perspective may attempt together to identify, for their own benefit, sufficient positive reasons for continuing to hold a certain belief – positive reasons for maintaining that this belief is superior to all competing beliefs. But this sort of apologetics, which might be labeled *intra-system communal positive apologetics*, does not differ for our purposes in any significant way from personal positive apologetics. Specifically, the primary goal in

each case is internal support – is to help bolster belief already held. Accordingly, since our assessment of personal positive apologetics will apply directly to this communal variant, I will say no more explicitly about the latter.

5. R.B. Kuiper in *The Voice of Authority*, G.W. Marston, ed. (Philadelphia: Presbyterian and Reformed Publishing House, 1960), p. 16.
6. See David Basinger, 'Bible Paradox: Does Revelation Challenge Logic?', *Journal of the Evangelical Theological Society* 30 (1987), pp. 205–13.
7. Even fideists, who are inclined to see an inverse relationship between rational support and true faith, don't deny that some form of personal positive apologetics – some attempt by an exclusivist to identify for herself her reasons for continued belief – is acceptable. For a fuller discussion of fideism, see Michael Peterson, William Hasker, Bruce Reichenbach and David Basinger, *Reason and Religious Belief*, 2nd edn (New York: Oxford University Press, 1998), pp. 49–53.
8. Alvin Plantinga, 'Pluralism: A Defense of Religious Exclusivism', in *The Philosophical Challenge of Religious Diversity*, Philip L. Quinn and Kevin Meeker, eds (New York: Oxford University Press, 2000), p. 189.
9. Ibid., p. 190.
10. Wilfred Cantwell Smith, *Religious Diversity* (New York: Harper and Row, 1976), p. 14.
11. Joseph Runzo, 'God, Commitment and Other Faiths: Pluralism vs. Relativism', *Faith and Philosophy* 5 (October 1988), p. 348.
12. John Hick, *An Interpretation of Religion* (New Haven: Yale University Press, 1989), p. 235.
13. John Hick, 'Religious Pluralism and Absolute Claims', in Leroy Rouner, ed., *Religious Pluralism* (Notre Dame: University of Notre Dame Press, 1984), p. 197.
14. See Chapter 4.
15. See Chapter 4. We need to add 'in principle' here because it is always possible to argue correctly that individual exclusivists display more or less transformation than do proponents of competing perspectives.
16. See Chapter 4.
17. See Chapter 4.
18. Paul J. Griffiths, 'An Apology for Apologetics', *Faith and Philosophy* 5 (October 1988), p. 400.
19. Ibid., p. 401.
20. While Griffiths speaks only of positive apologetics, the context makes it clear that the type of activity he has in mind is what I have labelled proselytizing positive apologetics. That is, what he is advocating is not simply that exclusivists attempt to discover for themselves reasons for considering their beliefs correct but that they attempt to convince their epistemic competitors to agree.
21. Ibid., p. 403.
22. Ibid., pp. 403–404.
23. It may also be true that those fideists who believe there to be an inverse relationship between faith and reason would be reticent to engage in proselytizing activity based on rational considerations – to offer arguments designed to convince others of their need to 'convert'. See again, Peterson et al., pp. 49–53.
24. See Chapter 3.
25. Alston and Plantinga make even stronger claims. For instance, not only does Alston grant 'that religious pluralism should diminish the confidence one has in the reliability of [the Christian belief-forming practice]', he acknowledges that 'one's justification for engaging in [the Christian belief-forming practice] is diminished by religious pluralism' ('Religious Diversity and Perceptual Knowledge of God', in *The Philosophical Challenge of Religious Diversity*, p. 205). And Plantinga maintains that for many or most exclusivists the reality of religious diversity 'directly reduces the level of confidence or degree of belief in the proposition in question' (Plantinga, 'Pluralism: A Defense of Religious Exclusivism', p. 189).
26. I have already argued that while exclusivists cannot demonstrate on grounds common to all that transformational parity is not a reality, they can personally deny justifiably that such parity actually exists. See Chapter 4 for a more detailed discussion of this point.

Chapter 7

Diversity and Teaching

As already noted, I have taught at least 8,000 students over the last 27 years. And while my teaching load is heavier than most – I have, until recently, taught not only four traditional undergraduate courses per semester but also numerous evening graduate/adult education classes interspersed throughout the year – most philosophers spend the majority of their time in classroom-related activities.

The purpose of this chapter is to share what I see as the appropriate impact of epistemic diversity – the fact that sincere, equally knowledgeable individuals differ on almost every issue that philosophers discuss – on classroom teaching. After defending the general contention that the reality of epistemic diversity is a sufficient reason for the philosopher *qua* teacher to keep her personal opinion out of the classroom, I will argue specifically that this holds even for the religious exclusivist who believes she ought to share the truth with others.[1]

It is important to note that I am claiming no necessary connection between my position on the standard questions related to religious diversity discussed in earlier chapters and my thoughts on classroom pedagogy. It is possible for someone to agree with everything I've said up to this point and justifiably disagree with the pedagogical claims I am about to make or vice versa. However, teaching for me is not simply a way of supporting myself while I'm 'doing my philosophy'. I not only enjoy teaching but also want to be an effective teacher since I think that the effective philosophy instructor has the potential to affect greatly the lives of his or her students. So I am always interested in exploring how I can create the best learning environment possible in the philosophy classroom.

The Case for Neutralism

Most who teach in college and university settings hold definite opinions on most of the significant issues that arise in their areas of expertise. Moreover, due to their training and experience, most normally feel that their views on such issues are thoughtful and well-informed and, accordingly, are quite willing to share these views with others. Should professors, however, do so in the classroom? Should they openly share their own perspectives with students? Answers to this question generally fall into two basic categories. Proponents of advocacy feel that it is certainly permissible, if not desirable, for the professor to make her own views clear to students, while proponents of neutralism argue that it is generally best for the professor not to do so.

The argument for neutralism begins with the reality of pervasive epistemic diversity – with the obvious fact that many people disagree on many issues. Now, of course, not all disagreements need be viewed as troublesome for our present purposes. The fact that Sam and George report a different account of the ball game loses significance when we discover that George is three years old and Sam is an ex-referee. The fact that Mary and Sue report seeing a different colour no longer bothers us when we discover that Sue is colour-blind. And the fact that John's report of an accident differs greatly from Carl's loses much of its impact when we learn that John is a habitual liar. Such disagreements are not problematic because the people making these rival claims are not epistemic peers – are not in the same position to comprehend or assess the truth.

However, even among those who are seemingly sincere and equally knowledgeable, significant disagreements on most important questions – including, as we have seen, most important religious questions – arise. And it seems to me that this has very significant implications for what occurs in the college or university classroom. As has already been noted, many, if not most, of the students who enter college or university classrooms have what I will label 'bestowed beliefs'. That is, many, if not most, did not acquire their most basic religious, moral, and social beliefs on the basis of a conscious line of reasoning. They did not consciously assess the evidence for and against these beliefs before deciding initially to affirm them. Nor do they continue to affirm such beliefs on the basis of a conscious assessment of the 'evidence'.

This is not to say students don't possess what they view as good reasons for continuing to affirm their beliefs. They can list many reasons why they believe, for instance, that God exists or abortion is wrong. However, most don't hold such beliefs primarily on the basis of such reasons. Rather, they usually hold their beliefs either because these beliefs were affirmed by an authority figure – for example, a parent or teacher or religious leader – or because such beliefs just seem obviously true, much as it seems obviously true to them on certain occasions that they are seeing a tree or sitting in a classroom.

That this is so, in and of itself, need not be viewed as problematic. All of us at times quite appropriately accept what 'authorities' tell us is true. And I agree in general with those who argue that, to avoid infinite regression, it is necessary in most significant discussions to assume the truth of certain propositions. In fact, as noted in an earlier chapter, it seems to me quite plausible to believe that we possess certain belief-forming faculties that often simply produce in us our religious, moral, or social beliefs in much the same fashion that other faculties produce our visual or auditory beliefs.[2] In short, we are under no obligation to automatically give up or even question our basic beliefs just because they are not grounded in some conscious line of reasoning.

However, students (and others) who respond to important issues primarily on the basis of beliefs acquired in this non-reflective manner often display two significant tendencies. First, they frequently feel that the answers to important religious, moral, or social questions are quite obvious and straightforward and, thus, view serious attempts to analyse critically such issues as unnecessary or counterproductive – that is, as polemic attempts to water down the truth or generate confusion.

This is not to say that such individuals do not, themselves, sometimes employ rational argumentation. However, they seldom do so to find the truth. Rational argumentation is used almost solely to defend or clarify the truth. For example, it is not at all uncommon for those who have a non-reflective foundation for believing that abortion is wrong to consider and utilize only those forms of rational argumentation that support their position.

Second, those whose basic beliefs have a non-reflective basis often consider those who don't agree with them – for example, those who don't believe in God or are pro-choice – to be at best uninformed or at worst insincere and, thus, as persons whose views need not be taken seriously.

However, as those of us who are professors are in a very good position to know, the answers to significant religious, ethical and social issues are almost never obvious and straightforward. In fact, we know that, as a general rule, the more such issues are seriously considered, the more complex they become. And we know that sincerity and competence seldom lie with those on just one side of the issue.

Accordingly, students who exhibit the tendencies in question are actually in a somewhat precarious position. They possess firmly held beliefs and are willing to defend them. However, usually they do not really understand what they believe. Hence, they are usually not in a position to engage seriously in meaningful discussions on the important issues of our day.

Now, of course, there may well be contexts in which a meaningful discussion is legitimately not the primary goal. Small children may at times simply need to be told what to believe or how to behave. And some worship services may not be an appropriate context in which to discuss alternative interpretations of important theological concepts. However, in those contexts where a primary goal is a search for truth, meaningful discussion is necessary. Thus, since I believe that a search for truth (or at least clarity) should be a primary goal in every college or university, I naturally believe that every college or university ought to attempt consciously to foster the conscious belief assessment necessary to help students understand what they actually do believe and why they believe it.

However, is neutralism – the withholding of personal perspectives by the professor – always (or generally) the best way to accomplish this goal? I obviously don't believe neutralism is *always* the most desirable way to approach controversial issues *outside* the classroom. For instance, I am, at present *advocating* a position on a debatable question. But I am presently addressing those who are well aware of the various competing perspectives on the issue at hand. And I agree with those who claim that advocacy is perhaps the best way to stimulate additional belief assessment in discussions between epistemic peers.

Students, however, are seldom epistemic peers. Some upper-level students may come to recognize the pluralistic nature of the key issues in their disciplines. Some may even develop the personal strength and intellectual tools necessary to grapple seriously and meaningfully with alternative ideas. As this occurs, it becomes more acceptable for professors to share their own views since classroom discussion can then start to become a 'meeting of the minds'.

Most students, though, come to class unaware of, and ill-equipped to deal with, the pervasive pluralism related to the basic issues in their disciplines. Thus, for most students, I believe that a neutral pedagogical approach is most appropriate. It forces them to begin thinking on their own and helps them develop the tools necessary to make their way through the various options. In other words, with respect to these students, I agree with John Stuart Mill:

> Diversity of opinion among men of equal ability, and who have taken equal pains to arrive at the truth ... should of itself be a warning to a conscientious teacher that he has no right to impose his opinion authoritatively upon the youthful mind ... The pupil should not be addressed as if his religion has been chosen for him, but as one who will have to choose it for himself.[3]

General Concerns

Proponents of advocacy, though, will surely remain unconvinced. First, some might grant that the reality of pervasive epistemic diversity does require students to engage in serious belief assessment – that some expanded version of Basinger's Rule does apply in the classroom – but question whether this is best accomplished by having the professor refrain from sharing her perspective. The role of the professor, it might be acknowledged, is to cultivate in the student the capacity for critical questioning. And, of course, it is extremely improbable that this can be accomplished if the professor's ultimate goal is to convince students that her perspective on all issues is the right one. However, if the professor has fostered a sense of open collegiality in the classroom, surely she can present various sides of an issue and then at the end simply share what is openly identified as her own personal opinion without dampening her students' desire for critical inquiry. Might it not be, in fact, that sharing her own perspective will better stimulate students to formulate and share their own perspectives?

As I have noted already, I am certainly not categorically opposed to professors having positions on issues and being willing to share them. However, I doubt that any form of 'professorial sharing' will foster significant belief reassessment in the typical college or university classroom. A professor may attempt to create an atmosphere of collegiality in the classroom, an atmosphere in which everyone, the professor included, is free to voice her opinion. But my experience has been that most students remain uneasy in such a context. Students don't mind disagreeing with each other; they sense that they normally stand on equal intellectual footing. And they often don't mind disagreeing with a professor in private discussions. Many students, though, do feel uneasy publicly espousing their views when they know the professor will be sharing hers later. Since the professor is perceived to be more knowledgeable, students often fear they will appear foolish if they have affirmed a perspective different from the one that they will later learn the professor holds.

More importantly, though, I question whether the majority of students will engage in belief assessment as seriously as they might if they know that the professor is going to be sharing her perspective at the end of the discussion. Some may not be affected. However, many, if not most, students have been conditioned by their culture to wait for the answer to dilemmas or problems. They have little experience in attempting to gain ownership of their own beliefs. Moreover, many come to class with little desire to grapple with intellectual tensions. Thus, no matter how clearly and emphatically the professor maintains that her own opinion should not be viewed as the answer and/or should not deter students from making a serious attempt to re-evaluate the beliefs they hold, many students, I fear, will simply wait for the professor to share her opinion and then adopt it.

Other critics have argued that neutralism itself is inherently dangerous. Stanley Hauerwas, for example, maintains that such an approach to teaching 'can too easily become a formula for intellectual cowardice and self-deception if it results in the assumption that as teachers we are released from the necessity of exposing our views to the critical response of students'.[4]

If the scope of Hauerwas' comments is broadened, he is right. Each professor, in her role as a 'professional thinker', does have the responsibility to expose her views to critical response. She especially has the responsibility to expose her views to critical assessment by her academic peers. It may even be true that she should invite student response in some manner.

However, I certainly don't believe that for a professor to refrain from exposing her views to undergraduates in the classroom normally demonstrates 'intellectual cowardice'. Most undergraduates are unable to challenge seriously the perspectives of their professors. Not only are these students generally less knowledgeable, they also are generally in no position in the classroom to engage in a fair debate. The professor may solicit critical feedback. But it is the professor who decides when the discussion should end and has 'the last word'. Furthermore, since all individuals enjoy presenting their beliefs in a context where they are assured of victory, it seems to me that sharing her beliefs in the classroom is one of the most tempting things for any professor to do. To *refrain* from doing so is for most actually the much more difficult task.

Stanley Hauerwas has also argued that neutralism can be incompatible with moral growth. This pedagogical approach, he declares, can keep a professor from 'trying to shape the lives of [her] students in a manner that might change their image of what they are or should be about'. That is, it can keep her from 'trying to change a student's fundamental moral stance'.

It encourages a professor, rather, to 'more or less leave students morally exactly the way we found them – that is, people who pride themselves on their autonomy, who are increasingly aware that all moral positions are "relative" or "subjective" since they are matters of choice'.[5]

There may be existent forms of neutralism to which this criticism rightly applies. However, Hauerwas' comments present no serious challenge to my position, for the form of neutralism I am advocating is not value-neutral. It is true that a professor utilizing my suggested pedagogical approach will want students to become increasingly aware of the various perspectives on issues; she will want them to develop some intellectual autonomy. However, this in no sense entails that she espouses relativism or considers intellectual autonomy the highest goal. Her primary goal, rather, will be to have students move beyond unreflective thought and commitment – to have them take some ownership of their beliefs. Accordingly, there is an important sense in which she will be 'trying to shape the lives of [her] students in a manner that might change their image of what they are or should be about'. In fact, one of my basic goals at present is to argue that the form of neutralism I am advocating is one of the best ways to do so.

Still other critics have argued that even if neutralism in the classroom is desirable, it is, in principle, impossible to achieve. Everyone, it is claimed, views reality through cultural lenses. That is, everyone (including every professor) exists in a cultural (socio-religious-moral) context that shapes the way she views reality and, accordingly, presents any body of material in the classroom. Hence, it is deceptive for a professor to make students believe they are ever really getting an objective analysis of all sides of an issue.[6]

There are actually two questions here: can the professor be totally objective and, if not, can the professor actually keep her perspective from showing? With respect to the first, I am willing to grant that total objectivity (however defined) is impossible. However, it doesn't follow from this that some discussions of given topics cannot be more objective than others. For example, although no discussion of abortion can be free from cultural bias, it does not follow that some discussions cannot help us see the key areas of controversy or the key metaphysical assumptions at stake more clearly, and in a less biased manner, than others. And the form of classroom neutrality I am defending pertains only to this latter type of objectivity – maintains only that the professor should attempt to refrain from sharing her perspective to the extent possible.

Moreover, it has been my personal experience that this can be accomplished quite successfully. For instance, although I'm sure I'm not totally objective in the classroom, I continue to have students who have taken my classes tell me (by way of formal evaluation and personal discussion) that they could never determine which of the perspectives I shared was really mine.[7]

It might also be argued that my form of neutralism places too high a premium on rational thought. Specifically, some might maintain with Alvin Plantinga that while the goal of the neutralist seems to be 'to see what can be established (or at least made plausible) using only the light of "natural, empirical reason" ', our goal should actually be to 'reach as much as [we] can of the full-fledged, full-orbed truth about the matter at hand', and that we should, accordingly, 'use all of [our] resources, everything [we] know, including what [we] know by faith'.[8]

In response, it is important to note that I have not argued that the proper use of reason *is* a sufficient basis for truth. I have not even argued that reason is a necessary condition for truth. It is compatible with my form of neutralism, for example, to grant that we possess innate knowledge or that we can acquire accurate information about reality through non-empirical channels – for example, through divine revelation. My argument is only that pervasive pluralism makes conscious belief assessment essential for students and that a neutral pedagogical approach is generally the best way to encourage students to engage in this important activity.

Finally, it might be argued that my form of neutralism has the potential to create in students a state of permanent confusion. For example, it might be argued that an objective assessment of controversial religious issues – for instance, an objective assessment of the various perspectives on the question of God's existence or the eternal destiny of humankind – could leave the student so unsure of what is true that she simply decides that truth in this area cannot be found and thus loses interest in further consideration of issues of this sort.

The tension to which this challenge points is very real. The line between a Socrates and a sophist – that is, between the seeker after truth and the sceptic – is very fine indeed. However, I do not see this tension as undermining my position.

It should first be noted that the type of neutrality I am proposing does not necessarily produce uncommitted sceptics. It might just as well, and is perhaps more likely to, produce critically committed students – that is, students who are committed, but have a clearer sense of why they hold the beliefs they do and exhibit an epistemological humility that keeps them from thinking they alone have the whole truth.

Furthermore, we must keep in mind that advocacy also runs the risk of creating cynical, sceptical students. For instance, many students take classes from more than one professor in a given department. But few departments contain professors who affirm the same positions on all important issues, and an encounter with rival 'authorities' can itself also be so confusing and frustrating that it points the student toward relativism or cynicism.

Hence, the best way to counteract and avoid cynicism and relativism, as I see it, is not by avoiding a neutrality that highlights diversity. It is, rather, to acknowledge diversity from the beginning and give the students the tools to deal creatively and critically with the alternatives.

Moreover, even if my form of neutralism does at times diminish the commitment and zealousness in some students, this isn't necessarily in all cases a negative consequence. Our world has no shortage of committed zealots. When former Nazi Albert Speer was asked how educated, non-mean-spirited persons could have cooperated with the Nazi atrocities, he answered: 'We were taught to never question'.[9] What our world does not need is more non-reflective commitment. What is needed, I believe, is more thoughtful, self-critical commitment.[10]

Religious Concerns

There is, though, one additional concern that I want to discuss in greater detail. It should be clear that the type of pedagogical neutralism I am proposing in no sense requires the professor to avoid classroom discussion of religious issues or religious perspectives on controversial topics. In fact, this approach does not even prohibit a professor from spending the majority of class time doing so. To affirm the type of neutralism in question is to say only that whatever issues are discussed in the classroom – including whatever religious issues are discussed – should be approached in as neutral (objective) a manner as possible.

However, might not a neutral discussion of religious issues or perspectives in the classroom generate a serious personal tension for the professor who is a religious exclusivist? Most professors, whether they are religious exclusivists or not, believe in principle in the open-minded pursuit of truth. They believe in principle that they should help students determine what they really believe – that is, help them develop convictions that are truly their own. But what of those cases in which the issue discussed is one on which the professor, as a religious exclusivist, not only holds a very firm opinion, but also believes it to be of vital practical importance that others agree and/or comes from a religious perspective that mandates that she share the truth whenever possible?

Let us consider, for instance, a cluster of common questions related to abortion. Is abortion justifiable when a woman's physical or emotional well-being is threatened by a pregnancy? Is abortion justifiable as a form of birth control? Is abortion as a method of gender selection justifiable? It is clearly possible for a professor not only to have strongly held exclusivistic religious convictions on such issues but also a personal desire to convince others to agree with her. In fact, she might believe, for reasons stated in the last chapter, that she is obligated to do so.

Doesn't my form of neutralism, however, not only prohibit her from sharing her own perspective on these issues in the classroom, but actually encourage (if not obligate) her to present the various perspectives on such issues, including those with which she strongly disagrees, in an objective manner? And might not such a presentation eventuate in a number of students affirming positions incompatible with her own?

In other words, to generalize, might not the practice of my form of neutralism place the professor who is a religious exclusivist in the very uncomfortable position of deliberately lending credence – by the very nature of her objective presentation – to perspectives on issues with respect to which she believes it important that only her perspective be held? Might not her 'neutrality' in fact be the catalyst for some students to switch their commitment from what she sees as the correct perspective?

The answer to each of these questions, I believe, is yes. To be neutral in the classroom can indeed create a context in which some students come to hold beliefs the professor considers not only to be false but also to have negative practical consequences. The professor who firmly believes, for instance, that abortion as a form of contraception is wrong might well find that some students, given an objective, neutral presentation of the relevant arguments, come to hold that just the opposite is true. So the tension in question can be quite real.

We must, though, keep a number of things in mind. First, for a professor to remain neutral in the sense I am outlining is not for the professor to keep the perspective she affirms, along with all accompanying support, out of the discussion. It is only for her to keep from the students to the extent possible the fact that this is her perspective. So if the support for her position is indeed the strongest, as she believes, this may well come through, apart from personal testimonial intervention on her part.

Second, we are in this context talking only about classroom discussions of issues on which the professor agrees there are justifiable positions other than her own. Hence, for instance, if a professor believes not only that the claim that the Holocaust really didn't occur is false but also that no one can justifiably disagree, then she is not, given my form of neutralism, obligated to present in a neutral fashion the various perspectives on this question.

However, we need to be careful here to distinguish between the claim that a religious exclusivist is justified in believing that her perspective on a given issue – for instance, the eternal destiny of humankind – is superior and the claim that no one can justifiably disagree. My perspective allows a professor to reject neutralism in the latter case, but not the former. That is, I'm claiming that while a professor need not be neutral when 'all' agree there exists only one justifiable perspective on an issue, a professor should remain neutral with respect to any issue on which there exists more than one justifiable perspective, even if she herself is convinced (even justifiably) that one of these perspectives is clearly superior.

Or, to state this important point differently, the fact that a professor is justified in believing she is right is not, I am maintaining, a justifiable basis for her, in her role as a professor in the classroom, to attempt to convince others that she is right. Rather, since I believe that the classroom is a context in which a student has the right to have access to all of the relevant information available to the instructor, it is my contention that when the professor must acknowledge that there exist justifiable perspectives other than her own, she is then ethically obligated to share these perspectives also.

This can, indeed, be very uncomfortable for those professors who believe firmly that their perspectives on controversial issues are correct. In fact, it has been my experience that it can become so uncomfortable that professors are sometimes tempted to promote their own perspectives under the guise of objectivity.

I do not see any of this, however, as a justification for proselytizing in the classroom. Even if my claim that neutralism is the best way to help develop critical thinkers is rejected, the professor, as I see it, is not justified in attempting in the classroom setting to convince students to accept her perspective when she recognizes what her students do not: that there are others as well-informed as she who justifiably see things differently. And I personally believe neutralism of the form I have outlined to be the best way to avoid explicit or implicit proselytization of this sort.

Conclusion

It is important that I emphasize again in closing that my argument for neutralism in the classroom is related to, but separable from, Basinger's Rule – from my claim that in the face of peer conflict the exclusivist is obligated to assess her beliefs. Specifically, I have not argued that neutralism is the only justifiable pedagogical approach, even for those who endorse Basinger's Rule. However, I have argued that neutralism is the best way to encourage students to engage in the sort of belief assessment I think is so necessary in the increasingly diverse, complex world in which we live.

Notes

1. While my argument for pedagogical neutrality is directed primarily at undergraduate teaching, the type of neutrality I am defending is also, I believe, normally appropriate at the graduate level.
2. See, for instance, Alvin Plantinga, 'Justification and Theism', *Faith and Philosophy* 4 (October 1987), pp. 403–26.
3. John Stuart Mill, in *Mill's Essays on Literature and Society*, J.B. Schneewind, ed. (New York: Collier-Macmillan, 1965), p. 399.
4. Stanley Hauerwas, *The Peaceable Kingdom* (Notre Dame: University of Notre Dame Press, 1983), p. xii.
5. Stanley Hauerwas, 'How Christian Universities Contribute to the Corruption of Youth: Church and University in a Confused Age', *Faculty Dialogue* 6 (Spring–Summer, 1986), p. 84.
6. See, for example, Richard Perkins, 'The Place of Ideology in Christian Liberal Arts: Why We Need More "Ought" and Less "Is"', *Faculty Dialogue* 7 (Fall–Winter, 1986–87), pp. 53–70.
7. I recently had a graduate student tell me that when he and his friends were in my undergraduate classes, they would sometimes argue in the dorm after class about which perspective presented was really mine.
8. Alvin Plantinga, 'Sheehan's Shenanigans: How Theology Becomes Tomfoolery', *Reformed Journal* (April 1987), p. 24.
9. As cited in Elias Baumgarten, 'Ethics in Academic Professions', *Journal of Higher Education* 53 (1982), p. 288.
10. Much of this argument for neutrality first appeared in 'Neutrality in the College Classroom: A Defense', *Faculty Dialogue* 12 (1989), p. 79–92, co-authored with my brother, Randall Basinger. Used with permission.

Selected Readings

Adler, Mortimer Jerome, *Truth in Religion: The Plurality of Religions and the Unity of Truth* (New York: Macmillan Publishing Company, 1992).

Alston, William, 'Response to Hick', *Faith and Philosophy* 14 (1997), pp. 287–8.

Byrne, Peter, 'John Hick's Philosophy of World Religions', *Scottish Journal of Theology* 35 (1982), pp. 289–301.

Corliss, Richard, 'A Study of Hick and an Alternative', *Religious Studies* 22 (1986), pp. 235–48.

D'Costa, Gavin, *Christian Uniqueness Reconsidered: the Myth of a Pluralistic Theology of Religions* (Maryknoll, NY: Orbis, 1990).

——, *Theology and Religious Pluralism: The Challenge of Other Religions* (London: Blackwell, 1986).

DiNoia, J.A., *The Diversity of Religions: A Christian Perspective* (Washington, DC: Catholic University of America Press, 1992).

Dupuis, Jacques, *Toward a Christian Theology of Religious Pluralism* (Maryknoll, NY: Orbis, 1999).

Eddy, Paul R., 'Religious Pluralism and the Divine: Another Look at John Hick's Neo-Kantian Proposal', *Religious Studies* 30 (1994), pp. 467–78.

Griffiths, Paul, *An Apology for Apologetics: A Study in the Logic of Interreligious Dialogue* (Maryknoll, NY: Orbis, 1991).

Griffiths, Paul and Delmas Lewis, 'On Grading Religions, Seeking Truth, and Being Nice to People – A Reply to Professor Hick', *Religious Studies* 19 (1983), pp. 75–80.

Hewitt, Harold, ed., *Problems in the Philosophy of Religion: Critical Studies of the Work of John Hick* (New York: St. Martin's Press, 1991).

Hick, John, *God Has Many Names* (Philadelphia: Westminster Press, 1982).

Hick, John, *Problems of Religious Pluralism* (New York: St. Martin's Press, 1985).

Hick, John, *An Interpretation of Religion: Human Responses to the Transcendent* (New Haven and London: Yale University Press, 1989).

Hick, John, 'The Epistemological Challenge of Religious Pluralism', *Faith and Philosophy* 14 (1997), pp. 277–86.

Knitter, Paul, *No Other Name? A Critical Survey of Christian Attitudes toward World Religions* (Maryknoll, NY: Orbis, 1985).

Mavrodes, George I., 'A Response to John Hick', *Faith and Philosophy* 14 (1997), pp. 289–94.

Netland, George A., 'Professor Hick on Religious Pluralism', *Religious Studies* 22 (1986), pp. 249–61.

Netland, Harold, *Dissonant Voices: Religious Pluralism and the Question of Truth* (Grand Rapids, MI: William B. Eerdmans Press, 1991).

Plantinga, Alvin, 'Ad Hick', *Faith and Philosophy* 14 (1997), pp. 295–98.

Senor, Thomas D., ed., *The Rationality of Belief and the Plurality of Faith* (Ithaca: Cornell University Press, 1995).

Sharma, Arvind, *God, Truth and Reality: Essays in Honour of John Hick* (New York: St. Martin's Press, 1993), pp. 210–20.

Smart, Ninian, *Buddhism and Christianity: Rivals and Allies* (Honolulu: University of Hawaii Press, 1993).

Smith, Wilfred Cantwell, *Towards a World Theology* (Philadelphia: Westminster Press, 1981).

Tracy, David, *Blessed Rage for Order: The New Pluralism in Theology* (Chicago: University of Chicago Press, 1995).

Twiss, Sumner B., 'The Philosophy of Religious Pluralism: A Critical Appraisal of Hick and his Critics', *The Journal of Religion* 70 (1990), pp. 533–68.

Vroom, Hendrik, *Religion and the Truth: Philosophical Reflections and Perspectives* (Grand Rapids, MI: William B. Eerdmans, 1989).

Ward, Keith, 'Truth and the Diversity of Religions', *Religious Studies* 26 (1990), pp. 6–11.

Wiggins, James B., *In Praise of Religious Diversity* (London: Routledge, 1996).

Index